Introduction to MATLAB for Engineers and Scientists

Delores M. Etter

Department of Electrical and Computer Engineering
University of Colorado, Boulder

An Alan R. Apt Book

Prentice Hall, Upper Saddle River, New Jersey 07458

Library of Congress Cataloging–in–Publication Data
Etter, Delores M.
    Introduction to Matlab for Engineers and Scientists
    Delores M. Etter.
        p. cm.
    "An Alan R. Apt book."
    Includes bibliographical references and index.
    ISBN 0-13-519703-1
CIP Data Available

Publisher: Alan Apt
Editor-in-Chief: Marcia Horton
Project Manager: Mona Pompili
Copy Editor: Shirley Michaels
Design Director: Amy Rosen
Designers: Meryl Poweski, Mona Pompili, Delores M. Etter
Production Coordinator: Donna Sullivan
Editorial Assistant: Shirley McGuire
Cover Graphic: Using the MATLAB Image Processing Toolbox, a Radon transform locates and high-
    lights density differences not visible in an X-ray of the lower spine. Provided by The MathWorks,
    Inc., Natick, MA.

In memory of my dearest Mother, Muerladene Janice Van Camp

© 1996 by Prentice-Hall, Inc.
Simon & Schuster / A Viacom Company
Upper Saddle River, New Jersey 07458

The author and publisher of this book have used their best efforts in preparing this book. These efforts include the development, research, and testing of the theories and programs to determine their
effectiveness. The author and publisher shall not be liable in any event for incidental or consequential
damages in connection with, or arising out of, the furnishing, performance, or use of these programs.

Printed in the United States of America

10 9 8 7 6 5 4 3 2

ISBN 0-13-519703-1

PRENTICE-HALL INTERNATIONAL (UK) LIMITED, *London*
PRENTICE-HALL OF AUSTRALIA PTY. LIMITED, *Sydney*
PRENTICE-HALL CANADA, INC., *Toronto*
PRENTICE-HALL HISPANOAMERICANA, S.A., *Mexico*
PRENTICE-HALL OF INDIA PRIVATE LIMITED, *New Delhi*
PRENTICE-HALL OF JAPAN, INC., *Tokyo*
SIMON & SCHUSTER ASIA PTE. LTD., *Singapore*
EDITORA PRENTICE-HALL DO BRASIL, LTDA., *Rio de Janeiro*

TRADEMARK INFORMATION

MATLAB is a registered
trademark of
The MathWorks, Inc.

Introduction to MATLAB for Engineers and Scientists

PRENTICE HALL MODULAR SERIES FOR ENGINEERING

Available now

Available in 1996

Preface

Engineers use computers to solve a variety of problems ranging from the evaluation of a simple function to solving a system of nonlinear equations. MATLAB has become the technical computing environment of choice of many engineers and scientists because it is a single interactive system that integrates numeric computation, symbolic computation, and scientific visualization. Because the MATLAB computing environment is the one that a new engineer is most likely to encounter in a job, it is a good choice for an introduction to computing for engineers. Therefore, this text was written to introduce engineering problem solving with the following objectives:

- to present a consistent **methodology for solving engineering problems**,
- to introduce the **computational and visualization capabilities of MATLAB**, the computing environment of choice of many practicing engineers and scientists, and
- to illustrate the problem-solving process with MATLAB through a variety of **engineering examples and applications**.

To accomplish these objectives, Chapter 1 presents a five-step process that is used in solving engineering problems, and Chapters 2–6 introduce the fundamental capabilities of MATLAB for solving engineering problems.

PREREQUISITES

No prior experience with the computer is assumed. The mathematical prerequisites are **college algebra and trigonometry**. Of course, the initial material can be covered much faster if the student has used other computer languages or software tools.

INTRODUCTION TO MATLAB

Many schools are using their introductory engineering courses to acquaint students with a variety of computer tools and languages. As a result, this text was developed as a brief introduction to MATLAB. Chapters 1–3 are necessary to solve most engineering problems, and Chapters 4–6 introduce additional topics, such as matrix inverses, symbolic mathematics, and numerical techniques for interpolation, curve fitting, integration, and differentiation. In a typical introductory course, this material can be covered in six weeks. a For semester or quarter course devoted entirely to engineering problem solving with MATLAB, we recommend the text *Engineering Problem Solving with MATLAB*, also written by Delores M. Etter. In addition to more extensive coverage of the numerical computing, symbolic computing, and plotting features of MATLAB, this expanded text contains additional topics, such as solutions to ordinary differential equations, matrix manipulations, matrix decomposition and factorization, and an introduction to the signals and systems toolbox.

PROBLEM-SOLVING METHODOLOGY

The **emphasis on engineering and scientific problem solving** is an important part of this text. Chapter 1 introduces a **five-step process for solving engineering problems** using the computer:

1. State the problem clearly.
2. Describe the input and output information.
3. Work a simple example by hand.
4. Develop an algorithm and convert it to MATLAB.
5. Test the solution with a variety of data.

To reinforce the development of problem-solving skills, each of these steps is identified each time that a complete solution is developed.

ENGINEERING AND SCIENTIFIC APPLICATIONS

Throughout the text, emphasis is placed on incorporating real-world engineering and scientific examples and problems. This emphasis is centered around a theme of **grand challenges,** which include

- prediction of weather, climate, and global change
- computerized speech understanding
- mapping of the human genome
- improvements in vehicle performance
- enhanced oil and gas recovery

Each chapter begins with a photograph and a discussion of some aspect of one of these grand challenges that provides a glimpse of some of the exciting and interesting areas in which engineers might work. The grand challenges are also referenced in many of the other examples and problems.

VISUALIZATION

The visualization of the information related to a problem and its solution is a critical component in understanding and developing the intuition necessary to be a creative engineer. Therefore, we have included a number of plots of data throughout the text to illustrate the relationships of the information needed to understand and solve specific problems.

SOFTWARE ENGINEERING CONCEPTS

Engineers and scientists are also expected to develop and implement **user-friendly** and **reusable** computer solutions. Learning software engineering techniques is therefore crucial to successfully developing these computer solutions. **Readability** and **documentation** are stressed in the development of programs. By using MATLAB, students are able to write **portable** code that can be transferred from one computer platform to another. Additional topics that relate to software engineering issues are discussed throughout the text and include issues such as the **software life cycle, maintenance, modularity, abstraction,** and **software prototypes**.

EXERCISES AND PROBLEMS

Learning any new skill requires practice at a number of different levels of difficulty. **Practice! problems** are short-answer questions that relate to the section of material just presented. Most sections are immediately followed by a set of Practice! problems so that students can determine if they are ready to continue to the next section. Complete solutions to all the Practice! problems are included at the end of the text.

Each chapter ends with a set of **end-of-chapter problems**. These are new problems that relate to a variety of engineering applications. The level of difficulty ranges from very straightforward to longer assignments. Engineering data sets are included for many of the problems to use in testing.

STUDENT AIDS

Margin notes are used to help the reader not only identify the important concepts, but also to easily locate specific topics. At the end of each chapter is a chapter summary that reviews the topics covered in the chapter and a MATLAB summary that lists all the special characters, commands, and functions that were defined in the chapter. In addition, a summary of the MATLAB functions discussed in this text is included at the end of the text.

INSTRUCTOR'S MANUAL

An **Instructor's Manual** is available which contains complete solutions to all the end-of-chapter problems. Also, transparency masters are included to assist in preparing lecture material.

ACKNOWLEDGMENTS

I appreciate the encouragement of Cleve Moler (Chairman of The MathWorks, Inc.) and Alan Apt (Senior Computer Science Editor) during the development of my

MATLAB texts. I also want to acknowledge the outstanding work of the publishing team at Prentice Hall, including Marcia Horton, Tom Robbins, Dan Kaveney, Gary June, Mona Pompili, Sondra Chavez, Alice Dworkin, and Mike Sutton. This text has been significantly improved by the suggestions and comments of the reviewers of *Engineering Problem Solving with* MATLAB. These reviewers included Randall Janka, The MITRE Corporation; Professor John A. Fleming, Texas A&M; Professor Jim Maneval, Bucknell University; Professor Helmuth Worbs, University of Central Florida; Professor Huseyin Abut, San Diego State University; Professor Richard Shiavi, Vanderbilt University; Captain Randy Haupt, U.S. Air Force Academy; Professor Zoran Gajic, Rutgers University; Professor Stengel, Princeton University; Professor William Beckwith, Clemson University; and Professor Juris Vagners, University of Washington. I also want to express my gratitude to my husband, a mechanical engineer, for his help in developing some of the engineering applications problems, and to my daughter, a veterinarian student, for her help in developing some of the DNA-related material and problems. Finally, I want to recognize the important contributions of the students in my introductory engineering courses for their feedback on the explanations, the examples, and the problems.

Delores M. Etter
Department of Electrical/Computer Engineering
University of Colorado, Boulder

Contents

6 Numerical Techniques

Grand Challenge: Enhanced Oil and Gas Recovery

Introduction to MATLAB for Engineers and Scientists

1

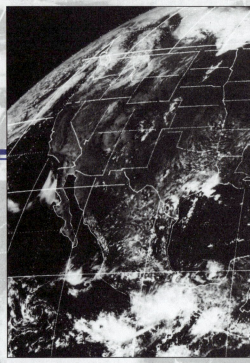

Courtesy of Texas Instruments Incorporated.

GRAND CHALLENGE:
Weather Prediction

Weather satellites provide a great deal of information to meteorologists who attempt
to predict the weather. Large volumes of historical weather data can also be analyzed
and used to test models for predicting weather. In general, meteorologists can do a
reasonably good job of predicting the overall weather patterns. However, local
weather phenomena, such as tornadoes, water spouts, and microbursts, are still very
difficult to predict. Even predicting heavy rainfall or large hail from thunderstorms
is often difficult. Although Doppler radar is useful in locating regions within storms
that could contain tornadoes or microbursts, the radar detects the events as they
occur and thus gives little time for issuing appropriate warnings to populated areas
or aircraft. Accurate and timely prediction of weather and associated weather phenomena is
still an elusive goal.

An Introduction to Engineering Problem Solving

OBJECTIVES

Although most of this text is focused on introducing you to the MATLAB computing environment and its capabilities, we begin by presenting a group of grand challenges—problems yet to be solved that will require technological breakthroughs in both engineering and science. One of the grand challenges includes the prediction of weather, which we used in the chapter opening discussion. Because most solutions to engineering problems use computers, we next describe computer systems with a discussion of both computer hardware and computer software. Solving engineering problems effectively with the computer also requires a design plan or procedure, and in this chapter we define a problem-solving methodology with five steps for describing a problem and then developing a solution.

1.1   Grand Challenges

Grand
challenges

Engineers solve real-world problems using scientific principles from disciplines that include computer science, mathematics, physics, and chemistry. It is this variety of subjects, and the challenge of real problems, that makes engineering so interesting and so rewarding. In this section we present a group of **grand challenges**—fundamental problems in science and engineering with broad potential impact. The grand challenges were identified by the Office of Science and Technology Policy in Washington, D.C., as part of a research and development strategy for high-performance computing. The following paragraphs briefly present some of these grand challenges and outline the types of benefits that will come with their solutions; additional discussion is presented at the beginning of each chapter. Just as the computer played an important part in the engineering achievements of the last thirty-five years, the computer will play an even greater role in solving problems related to these grand challenges.

Prediction of
weather, climate,
and global
change

The **prediction of weather, climate, and global change** requires that we understand the coupled atmosphere and ocean biosphere system. This includes understanding CO_2 dynamics in the atmosphere and ocean, ozone depletion, and climatological changes due to the releases of chemicals or energy. This complex interaction also includes solar interactions. A major eruption from a solar storm near a "coronal hole" (a venting point for the solar wind) can eject vast amounts of hot gases from the sun's surface toward the earth's surface at speeds of over a million miles per hour. This ejection of hot gases bombards the earth with x-rays and can interfere with communication and cause power fluctuations in power lines. Learning to predict changes in weather, climate, and global change involves collecting large amounts of data for study and developing new mathematical models that can represent the interdependency of many variables.

Computerized
speech
understanding

Computerized speech understanding could revolutionize our communication systems, but many problems are involved. Teaching a computer to understand words from a small vocabulary spoken by the same person is currently possible. However, to develop systems that are speaker-independent and that understand words from large vocabularies and from different languages is very difficult. Subtle changes in one's voice, such as those caused by a cold or stress, can affect the performance of speech recognition systems. Even assuming that the computer can recognize the words, it is not simple to determine their meaning. Many words are context-dependent and thus cannot be analyzed separately. Intonation, such as raising one's voice, can change a statement into a question. While there are still many difficult problems left to address in automatic speech recognition and understanding, exciting applications are everywhere. Imagine a telephone system that determines the languages being spoken and translates the speech signals so that each person hears the conversation in his or her native language.

Human genome
project

The goal of the **human genome project** is to locate, identify, and determine the function of each of the 50,000 to 100,000 genes that are contained in human DNA (deoxyribonucleic acid), which is the genetic material found in cells. The deciphering of the human genetic code will lead to many technical advances, in-

cluding the ability to detect most, if not all, of the over 4,000 known human genetic diseases, such as sickle-cell anemia and cystic fibrosis. However, deciphering the code is complicated by the nature of genetic information. Each gene is a
double-helix strand composed of base pairs (adenine bonded with thymine or
cytosine bonded with guanine) arranged in a step-like manner with phosphate
groups along the side. These base pairs can occur in any sequential order and
represent the hereditary information in the gene. The number of base pairs in
human DNA has been estimated to be around 3 billion. Because DNA directs
the production of proteins for all metabolic needs, the proteins produced by a
cell may provide a key to the sequence of base pairs in the DNA.

Improvements in vehicle performance

Substantial **improvements in vehicle performance** require more complex
physical modeling in the areas of fluid dynamic behavior for three-dimensional
flow fields and flow inside engine turbomachinery and ducts. Turbulence in
fluid flows impacts the stability and control, thermal characteristics, and fuel
performance of aerospace vehicles; modeling this flow is necessary for the
analysis of new configurations. The analysis of the aeroelastic behavior of vehicles also affects new designs. The efficiency of combustion systems is also related because attaining significant improvements in combustion efficiency requires understanding the relationships between the flows of the various
substances and the chemistry that causes the substances to react. Vehicle
performance is also being addressed through the use of onboard computers and
microprocessors. Transportation systems are currently being studied in which
cars have computers with small video screens mounted on the dash. The driver
enters the destination location, and the video screen shows the street names and
path to get from the current location to the desired location. A communication
network keeps the car's computer aware of any traffic jams so that it can automatically reroute the car if necessary. Other transportation research addresses
totally automated driving, with computers and networks handling all the control and information interchange.

Enhanced oil and gas recovery

Enhanced oil and gas recovery will allow us to locate the estimated 300
billion barrels of oil reserves in the U.S. Current techniques for identifying
structures likely to contain oil and gas use seismic techniques that can evaluate structures down to 20,000 feet below the surface. These techniques use a
group of sensors (called a sensor array) that is located near the area to be
tested. A ground shock signal is sent into the earth and is then reflected by the
different geological layer boundaries and is received by the sensors. Using sophisticated signal processing, the boundary layers can be mapped, and some
estimate can be made as to the materials in the various layers, such as sand-
stone, shale, and water. The ground shock signals can be generated in several
ways—a hole can be drilled, and an explosive charge can be exploded in the
hole; a ground shock can be generated by an explosive charge on the surface;
or a special truck that uses a hydraulic hammer can be used to pound the earth
several times per second. Continued research is needed to improve the resolution of the information and to find methods of production and recovery that
are economical and ecologically sound.

These grand challenges are only a few of the many interesting problems
waiting to be solved by engineers and scientists. The solutions to problems of

this magnitude will be the result of organized approaches that combine ideas and technologies. The use of computers and engineering problem-solving techniques will be a key element in the solution process.

1.2   Computing Systems

Before we begin discussing MATLAB, a brief discussion on computing is useful, especially for those who have not had prior experience with computers. A **computer** is a machine that is designed to perform operations that are specified with a set of instructions called a **program**. Computer **hardware** refers to the computer equipment, such as the keyboard, the mouse, the terminal, the hard disk, and the printer. Computer **software** refers to the programs that describe the steps that we want the computer to perform.

Program

COMPUTER HARDWARE

All computers have a common internal organization, as shown in Figure 1.1. The **processor** is the part of the computer that controls all the other parts. It accepts input values (from a device such as a keyboard) and stores them in the **memory**. It also interprets the instructions in a computer program. If we want to add two values, the processor will retrieve the values from memory and send them to the **arithmetic logic unit**, or ALU. The ALU performs the addition, and the processor then stores the result in memory. The processing unit and the ALU use internal memory composed of read-only memory (ROM) and random access memory (RAM) in their processing. Most data are stored in external memory or secondary memory using hard disk drives or floppy disk drives

Arithmetic logic unit

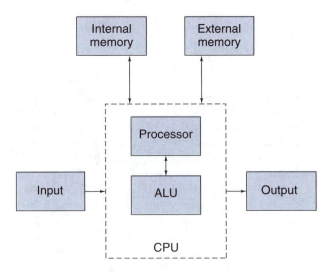

Figure 1.1 *Internal organization of a computer.*

that are attached to the processor. The processor and ALU together are called the **central processing unit** or CPU. A **microprocessor** is a CPU that is contained in a single integrated circuit chip that contains millions of components in an area smaller than a postage stamp.

We usually instruct the computer to print the values that it has computed on the terminal screen or on paper using a printer. Dot matrix printers use a matrix (or grid) of pins to produce the shape of a character on paper, whereas a laser printer uses a light beam to transfer images to paper. The computer can also write information to diskettes, which store the information magnetically. A printed copy of information is called a **hard copy**, and a magnetic copy of information is called an **electronic copy** or a soft copy.

PC

Computers come in all sizes, shapes, and forms. (See photos on the next page.) Personal computers **(PCs)** are small, inexpensive computers that are commonly used in offices, homes, and laboratories. PCs are also referred to as microcomputers. Their design is built around a microprocessor, such as the Intel 486 microprocessor, which can process millions of instructions per second (mips). Minicomputers are more powerful than microcomputers. Mainframes are even more powerful computers that are often used in businesses and research laboratories. A **workstation** is a minicomputer or mainframe computer that is small enough to fit on a desktop. **Supercomputers** are the fastest of all computers and can process billions of instructions per second. Because of their speed, supercomputers are capable of solving very complex problems that cannot be feasibly solved on other computers. Mainframes and supercomputers require special facilities and a specialized staff to run and maintain the computer systems.

The type of computer needed to solve a particular problem depends on the problem requirements. If the computer is part of a home security system, a microprocessor is sufficient; if the computer is running a flight simulator, a mainframe is probably needed. Computer **networks** allow computers to communicate with each other so that they can share resources and information. For example, ethernet is a commonly used local area network (LAN).

Network

COMPUTER SOFTWARE

Computer software contains the instructions or commands that we want the computer to perform. There are several important categories of software, including operating systems, software tools, and language compilers. Figure 1.2 illustrates the interaction among these categories of software and the computer hardware. We now discuss each of these software categories in more detail.

Operating Systems. Some software, such as the operating system, typically comes with the computer hardware when it is purchased. The operating system provides an interface between you (the user) and the hardware by providing a convenient and efficient environment in which you can select and execute the software on your system.

Operating systems also contain a group of programs called **utilities** that allow you to perform functions such as printing files, copying files from one

Courtesy of Johnson Space Center.

Courtesy of The Image Works.

Courtesy of Apple Computer Inc.

Courtesy of The Image Works.

Courtesy of CRAY Research.

Courtesy of IBM.

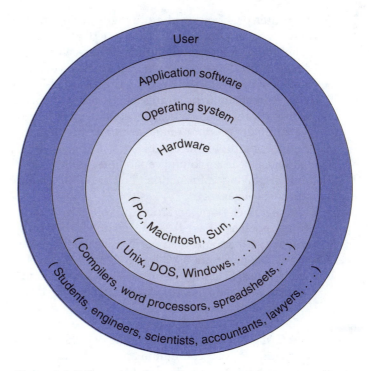

Figure 1.2 *Software interface to the computer.*

diskette to another, and listing the files that you have saved on a diskette. Although these utilities are common to most operating systems, the commands themselves vary from computer to computer. For example, to list your files using DOS (a disk operating system used mainly with PCs), the command is *dir*; to list your files with UNIX (a powerful operating system frequently used with workstations), the command is *ls*. Some operating systems simplify the interface with the operating system. Examples of user-friendly systems are the Macintosh environment and the Windows environment.

Because MATLAB programs can be run on many different platforms or hardware systems and because a specific computer can use different operating systems, it is not feasible to discuss the wide variety of operating systems that you might use while taking this course. We assume that your professor will provide the specific operating system information that you need to use the computers available at your university. This information is also contained in the operating system manuals.

Software Tools. Software tools are programs that have been written to perform common operations. For example, **word processors**, such as Microsoft Word and Word Perfect, are programs that have been written to help you enter and format text. Word processors allow you to move sentences and paragraphs and often have capabilities that allow you to enter mathematical equations and to check your spelling and grammar. Word processors are also used to enter

Word processor

computer programs and store them in files. Very sophisticated word processors allow you to produce well-designed pages that combine elaborate charts and graphics with text and headlines. These word processors use a technology called **desktop publishing**, which combines a very powerful word processor with a high-quality printer to produce professional-looking documents.

Spreadsheet

Spreadsheet programs are software tools that allow you to work easily with data that can be displayed in a grid of rows and columns. Spreadsheets were initially used for financial and accounting applications, but many science and engineering problems can be solved easily using spreadsheets. Most spreadsheet packages include plotting capabilities, so they can be especially useful in analyzing and displaying information. Lotus 1–2–3, Quattro Pro, and Excel are popular spreadsheet packages.

Database management

Another popular group of software tools are **database management** programs, such as dBase IV and Paradox. These programs allow you to store a large amount of data and then easily retrieve pieces of the data and format it into reports. Databases are used by large organizations, such as banks, hospitals, hotels, and airlines. Scientific databases are also used to analyze large amounts of data. Meteorology data is an example of scientific data that requires large databases for storage and analysis.

Computer-aided design

Computer-aided design (CAD) packages, such as AutoCAD, AutoSketch, and CADKEY, allow you to define objects and then manipulate them graphically. For example, you can define an object and then view it from different angles or observe a rotation of the object from one position to another.

Mathematical computation

MATLAB, Mathematica, MathCAD, and Maple are very powerful **mathematical computation** tools. Not only do these tools have very powerful mathematical commands, but they also provide extensive capabilities for generating graphs. This combination of computational power and visualization power make them particularly useful tools for engineers. In Chapter 2, we present the computing environment provided by MATLAB.

If an engineering problem can be solved using a software tool, it is usually more efficient to use the software tool than to write a program in a computer language to solve the problem. However, many problems cannot be solved using software tools, or a software tool may not be available on the computer system that must be used for solving the problem. Thus, we also need to know how to write programs using computer languages. The distinction between a software tool and a computer language is becoming less clear as some of the more powerful tools, such as MATLAB and Mathematica, include their own languages in additional to specialized operations.

Computer Languages. Computer languages can be described in terms of levels. Low-level languages or machine languages are the most primitive languages. **Machine language** is tied closely to the design of the computer hardware. Because computer designs are based on two-state technology (devices with two states, such as open or closed circuits, on or off switches, positive or negative charges), machine language is written using two symbols, which are usually rep-

Machine language

resented using the digits 0 and 1. Therefore, machine language is also a binary language, and the instructions are written as sequences of 0s and 1s called binary strings. Because machine language is closely tied to the design of the computer hardware, the machine language for a Sun computer is different from the machine language for a Silicon Graphics computer.

Assembly language

An **assembly language** is also unique to a specific computer design, but its instructions are written in English-like statements instead of binary. Assembly languages usually do not have very many statements; thus, writing programs in assembly language can be tedious. In addition, to use an assembly language, you must also know information that relates to the specific computer hardware. Instrumentation that contains microprocessors often requires that the programs operate very fast; thus, the programs are called **real-time programs**. These real-time programs are usually written in assembly language to take advantage of the specific computer hardware in order to perform the steps faster.

High-level languages

High-level languages are computer languages that have English-like commands and instructions and include languages such as C, Fortran, Ada, Pascal, COBOL and Basic. Writing programs in high-level languages is certainly easier than writing programs in machine language or in assembly language. However, a high-level language contains a large number of commands and an extensive set of **syntax** (or grammar) rules for using the commands. To illustrate the syntax and punctuation required by both software tools and high-level languages, we compute the area of a circle with a specified diameter in Table 1.1 using several different languages and tools. Notice both the similarities and the differences in this simple computation. Although we included C as a high-level language, many people like to describe C as a mid-level language because it allows access to low-level routines and is often used to define programs that are converted to assembly language.

Languages are also defined in terms of **generations**. The first generation of computer languages is machine language, the second generation is assembly language, and the third generation is high-level language. Fourth generation languages, also referred to as **4GLs,** have not been developed yet and are described only in terms of characteristics and programmer productivity. The fifth generation of languages is called natural languages. To program in a fifth-generation

Table 1.1 Comparison of Software Statements

Software	Example Statement
MATLAB	`area = pi*((diameter/2)^2);`
C	`area = 3.141593*(diameter/2)*(diameter/2);`
Fortran	`area = 3.141593*(diameter/2.0)**2`
Ada	`area := 3.141593*(diameter/2)**2;`
Pascal	`area := 3.141593*(diameter/2)*(diameter/2)`
BASIC	`let a = 3.141593*(d/2)*(d/2)`
COBOL	`compute area = 3.141593*(diameter/2)*(diameter/2).`

language, one would use the syntax of natural speech. Clearly, the implementation of a natural language would require the achievement of one of the grand challenges—computerized speech understanding.

Fortran (FORmula TRANslation) was developed in the mid-1950s for solving engineering and scientific problems. New standards updated the language over the years, and the current standard, Fortran 90, contains strong numerical computation capabilities, along with many of the new features and structures in languages such as C. **COBOL** (COmmon Business-Oriented Language) was developed in the late 1950s to solve business problems. **Basic** (Beginner's All-purpose Symbolic Instruction Code) was developed in the mid–1960s and was used as an educational tool; it is often included with the system software for a PC. **Pascal** was developed in the early 1970s and is widely used in computer science programs to introduce students to computing. **Ada** was developed at the initiative of the U.S. Department of Defense with the purpose of developing a high-level language appropriate to embedded computer systems that are typically implemented using microprocessors. The final design of the language was accepted in 1979. The language was named in honor of Ada Lovelace, who developed instructions for doing computations on an analytical machine in the early 1800s. **C** is a general-purpose language that evolved from two languages, BCPL and B, that were developed at Bell Laboratories in the late 1960s. In 1972, Dennis Ritchie developed and implemented the first C compiler on a DEC PDP–11 computer at Bell Laboratories. The language became very popular for system development because it was hardware independent. Because of its popularity in both industry and in academia, it became clear that a standard definition was needed. A committee of the American National Standards Institute (ANSI) was created in 1983 to provide a machine-independent and unambiguous definition of C. In 1989 the ANSI standard was approved.

Executing a Computer Program. A program written in a high-level language such as C must be translated into machine language before the instructions can be executed by the computer. A special program called a **compiler** is used to perform this translation. Thus, in order to be able to write and execute C programs on a computer, the computer's software must include a C compiler.

Compiler

If any errors (often called **bugs**) are detected by the compiler during compilation, corresponding error messages are printed. We must correct our program statements and then perform the compilation step again. The errors identified during this stage are called **compile errors** or compile-time errors. For example, if we want to divide the value stored in a variable called *sum* by 3, the correct expression in C is **sum/3**. If we incorrectly write the expression using the backslash, as in **sum\3**, we will have a compiler error. The process of compiling, correcting statements (or **debugging**), and recompiling must often be repeated several times before the program compiles without compiler errors. When there are no compiler errors, the compiler generates a program in machine language that performs the steps specified by the original C program. The original C program is referred to as the **source program**, and the machine language version is called an **object program**. Thus the source program and the object program specify the same steps, but the source program is specified in a high-level language, and the object program is specified in machine language.

Execution

Once the program has compiled correctly, additional steps are necessary to prepare the object program for **execution.** This preparation involves **linking** other machine language statements to the object program and then **loading** the program into memory. After this linking/loading, the program steps are then executed by the computer. New errors, called execution errors, run-time errors, or **logic errors,** may be identified in this stage; they are also called program bugs. Execution errors often cause termination of a program. For example, the program statements may attempt to perform a division by zero, which generates an execution error. Some execution errors do not stop the program from executing, but they cause incorrect results to be computed. These types of errors can be caused by programmer errors in determining the correct steps in the solutions and by errors in the data processed by the program. When execution errors occur because of errors in the program statements, we must correct the errors in the source program and then begin again with the compilation step. Even when a program appears to execute properly, we must check the answers carefully to be sure that they are correct. The computer will perform the steps precisely as we specify. If we specify the wrong steps, the computer will execute these wrong (but syntactically legal) steps and present us with an answer that is incorrect.

The processes of compilation, linking/loading, and execution are outlined in Figure 1.3. The process of converting an assembly language program to binary is performed by an **assembler** program, and the corresponding processes are called assembly, linking/ loading, and execution.

Executing a MATLAB Program. In the MATLAB environment, we can develop and execute programs, or scripts, that contain MATLAB commands. We can also execute a MATLAB command, observe the results, and then execute another MATLAB command that interacts with the information in memory, observe its results, and so on. This **interactive environment** does not require the formal compilation, linking/loading, and execution process that was described for high-level computer languages. However, errors in the syntax of a MATLAB command are detected

Interactive environment

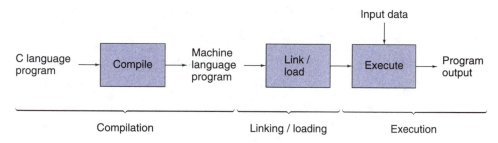

Figure 1.3 *Program compilation/linking/execution.*

when the MATLAB environment attempts to translate the command, and logic errors can cause execution errors when the MATLAB environment attempts to execute the command.

Software Life Cycle. In 1955, the cost of a typical computer solution was estimated to be 15% for the software development and 85% for the associated computer hardware. Over the years, the cost of the hardware has dramatically decreased, while the cost of the software has increased. In 1985, it was estimated that these numbers had essentially switched, with 85% of the cost for the software and 15% for the hardware. With the majority of the cost of a computer solution residing in the software development, a great deal of attention has been given to understanding the development of a software solution.

The development of a software project generally follows definite steps or cycles, which are collectively called the **software life cycle.** These steps typically include project definition, detailed specification, coding and modular testing, integrated testing, and maintenance. Data indicate that the corresponding percentages of effort involved can be estimated as shown in Table 1.2. From these estimates, it is clear that software maintenance is a significant part of the cost of a software system. This **maintenance** includes adding enhancements to the software, fixing errors identified as the software is used, and adapting the software to work with new hardware and software. The ease of providing maintenance is directly related to the original definition and specification of the solution because these steps lay the foundation for the rest of the project. The problem-solving process that we present in the next section emphasizes the need to define and specify the solution carefully before beginning to code or test it.

One of the techniques that has been successful in reducing the cost of software development both in time and in cost is the development of **software prototypes**. Instead of waiting until the software system is developed and then letting the users work with it, a prototype of the system is developed early in the life cycle. This prototype does not have all the functions required of the final software, but it allows the user to use it early in the lifecycle and to make desired modifications to the specifications. Making changes earlier in the life cycle is both cost-effective and time-effective. Because of its powerful commands and its graphics capabilities, MATLAB is especially effective in developing software prototypes. Once the MATLAB prototype is correctly performing the desired operations and the users are happy with the user/software interaction,

Maintenance

Software prototypes

Table 1.2 Software Life Cycle Phases	
Life Cycle	**Percent of Effort**
Definition	3%
Specification	15%
Coding and Modular Testing	14%
Integrated Testing	8%
Maintenance	60%

the final solution may be the MATLAB program, or the final solution may be converted to another language for implementation with a specific computer or piece of instrumentation.

As an engineer, it is very likely that you will need to modify or add additional capabilities to existing software. These modifications will be much simpler if the existing software is well-structured and readable and if the documentation that accompanies the software is up-to-date and clearly written. Even with powerful tools such as MATLAB, it is important to write well-structured and readable code. For these reasons, we stress developing good habits that make software more readable and self-documenting.

1.3   An Engineering Problem-Solving Methodology

Problem solving is a key part of not only engineering courses, but also courses in computer science, mathematics, physics, and chemistry. Therefore, it is important to have a consistent approach to solving problems. It is also helpful if the approach is general enough to work for all these different areas so that we do not have to learn a technique for mathematics problems, a different technique for physics problems, and so on. The problem-solving technique that we present works for engineering problems and can be tailored to solve problems in other areas as well. However, it does assume that we are using the computer to help solve the problem.

The process or methodology for problem solving that we will use throughout this text has **five steps:**

1. State the problem clearly.
2. Describe the input and output information.
3. Work the problem by hand (or with a calculator) for a simple set of data.
4. Develop a MATLAB solution.
5. Test the solution with a variety of data.

We now discuss each of these steps using data collected from a physics laboratory experiment. Assume that we have collected a set of temperatures from a sensor on a piece of equipment that is being used in an experiment. The temperature measurements are taken every 30 seconds, for 5 minutes, during the experiment. We want to compute the average temperature and we also want to plot the temperature values.

1.   PROBLEM STATEMENT

The first step is to state the problem clearly. It is extremely important to give a clear, concise problem statement to avoid any misunderstandings. For this example, the problem statement is the following:

Compute the average of a set of temperatures. Then plot the time and temperature values.

2.   INPUT/OUTPUT DESCRIPTION

The second step is to describe carefully the information that is given to solve the problem and then to identify the values to be computed. These items represent the input and the output for the problem and collectively can be called input/output or I/O. For many problems, a diagram that shows the input and output is useful. At this point the program is an "abstraction" because we are not defining the steps to determine the output; instead, we are only showing the information that is used to compute the output. The **I/O diagram** for this example follows:

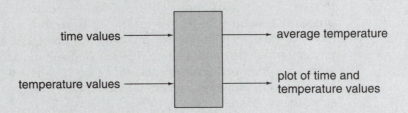

3.   HAND EXAMPLE

The third step is to work the problem by hand or with a calculator, using a simple set of data. This is a very important step and should not be skipped even for simple problems. This is the step in which you work out the details of the problem solution. If you cannot take a simple set of numbers and compute the output (either by hand or with a calculator), you are not ready to move on to the next step. You should reread the problem and perhaps consult reference material. For this problem, the only calculation is computing the average of a set of temperature values. Assume that we use the following data for the hand example:

time (minutes)	temperature (degrees F)
0.0	105
0.5	126
1.0	119

By hand, we compute the average to be $(105 + 126 + 119)/3$, or 116.6667 degrees F.

4.   MATLAB SOLUTION

Once you can work the problem for a simple set of data, you are then ready to develop an **algorithm,** a step-by-step outline of the problem solution. For simple problems such as this one, the algorithm can be written immediately using MATLAB commands. For more complicated problems, it may be necessary to write an outline of the steps and then decompose the steps into smaller steps that can be translated into MATLAB commands. One of the strengths of MATLAB is that its commands match very closely to the steps that we use to solve engineering problems. Thus, the process of determining the steps to solve the problem also determines the MATLAB commands. The next chapter discusses the details of the MATLAB commands used in the following solution, but observe that the MATLAB steps match closely to the solution steps from the hand example:

```
%    Compute average temperature and
%    plot the temperature data.
%
time = [0.0, 0.5, 1.0];
temps = [105, 126, 119];
average = mean(temps)
plot(time,temps),title('Temperature Measurements'),
xlabel('Time, minutes'),
ylabel('Temperature, degrees F'),grid
```

The words that follow percent signs are comments to help us in reading the MATLAB statements. If a MATLAB statement assigns or computes a value, it will also print the value on the screen if the statement does not end in a semicolon. Thus, the values of **time** and **temps** will not be printed because the statements that assign them values end with semicolons. The value of the average will be computed and printed on the screen because the statement that computes it does not end with a semicolon. Finally a plot of the time and temperature data will be generated.

5   TESTING

The final step in our problem-solving process is testing the solution. We should first test the solution with the data from the hand example because we have already computed the solution. When the previous statements are executed, the computer displays the following output:

```
average =
   116.6667
```

A plot of the data points is also shown on the screen. Because the average matches the one from the hand example, we now replace the hand data with the data from the physics experiment, giving the following program:

```
%  Compute average temperature and
%  plot the temperature data.
%
time = [0.0, 0.5, 1.0, 1.5, 2.0, 2.5, 3.0, . . .
        3.5, 4.0, 4.5, 5.0];
temps = [105, 126, 119, 129, 132, 128, 131, . . .
        135, 136, 132, 137];
average = mean(temps)
plot(time,temps),title('Temperature Measurements'),
xlabel('Time, minutes'),
ylabel('Temperature, degrees F'),grid
```

When these commands are executed, the computer displays the following output:

```
average =
   128.1818
```

The plot in Figure 1.4 is also shown on the screen.

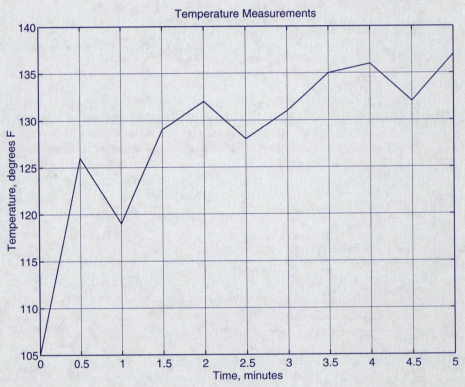

Figure 1.4 *Temperatures collected in physics experiment.*

The set of steps demonstrated in this example is used in developing the programs in the "Problem Solving Applied" sections in the chapters that follow.

CHAPTER SUMMARY

A set of grand challenges was presented to illustrate some of the exciting and difficult problems that currently face engineers and scientists. Because the solutions to most engineering problems, including the grand challenges, will involve the computer, we also presented a summary of the components of a computer system, from computer hardware to computer software. We also introduced a five-step problem-solving methodology that we will use to develop a computer solution to a problem. These five steps are as follows:

1. State the problem clearly.
2. Describe the input and output information.
3. Work the problem by hand (or with a calculator) for a simple set of data.
4. Develop a MATLAB solution.
5. Test the solution with a variety of data.

This process will be used throughout the text as we develop solutions to problems.

2

Courtesy of National Aeronautics and Space Administration.

GRAND CHALLENGE:
Vehicle Performance

Wind tunnels are test chambers built to generate precise wind speeds. Accurate scale models of new aircraft can be mounted on force-measuring supports in the test chamber, and then measurements of the forces on the model can be made at many different wind speeds and angles of the model relative to the wind direction. Some wind tunnels can operate at hypersonic velocities, generating wind speeds of thousands of miles per hour. The sizes of wind tunnel test sections vary from a few inches across to sizes large enough to accommodate a business jet. At the completion of a wind tunnel test series, many sets of data have been collected that can be used to determine the lift, drag, and other aerodynamic performance characteristics of a new aircraft at its various operating speeds and positions.

MATLAB *Environment*

OBJECTIVES

In this chapter we present the MATLAB environment, which is an interactive environment for numeric computation, data analysis, and graphics. After an introduction to the three types of MATLAB display windows, we discuss the ways of representing data as scalars, vectors, or matrices. A number of operators are presented for defining and computing new information. Commands are also presented for printing information and generating plots of information. Finally, we present an example that computes and plots the velocity and acceleration of an aircraft with an advanced turbo-prop engine.

2.1   Characteristics of the MATLAB Environment

**Matrix
Laboratory**

The MATLAB software was originally developed to be a "**Matrix Laboratory**." Today's MATLAB has capabilities far beyond the original MATLAB and is an interactive system and programming language for general scientific and technical computation. Its basic element is a matrix (which we discuss in detail in the next section). Because the MATLAB commands are similar to the way that we express engineering steps in mathematics, writing computer solutions in MATLAB is much quicker than writing computer solutions using a high-level language such as C or Fortran. In this section we explain the differences between the student version and the professional version of MATLAB, and we give you some initial workspace information.

STUDENT EDITION VERSION 4

The Student Edition Version 4 is very similar to the Professional Version 4 of MATLAB except for these features:

- Each vector is limited to 8192 elements.
- Each matrix is limited to a total of 8192 elements, with either the number of rows or columns limited to 32.
- Output can be printed using Windows, the Macintosh, and PostScript printing devices.
- Programs cannot dynamically link C or Fortran subroutines.
- A math coprocessor is strongly recommended but is not required.
- A Symbolic Math Toolbox and a Signals and Systems Toolbox are included with the student edition.

If you purchase the student edition of MATLAB, be sure to complete and return the registration card. As a registered student user, you are entitled to replacement of defective disks at no charge. You also qualify for a discount on upgrades to professional versions of MATLAB, and you will receive update information on MATLAB.

We assume that MATLAB is already installed on the computer that you are using. (If you have purchased the student edition of MATLAB, follow the installation instructions in the manual that accompanies the software.) The discussions and programs developed in this text will run properly using either the student edition or the professional version. We will assume that the input interaction uses a keyboard and a mouse.

MATLAB WINDOWS

Prompt

To begin MATLAB, select the MATLAB program from a menu in your operating system, or enter `matlab` with the keyboard. You should see the MATLAB **prompt** (`>> or EDU>>`), which tells you that MATLAB is waiting for you to enter a command. To exit MATLAB, use `quit or exit`.

**Display
windows**

MATLAB uses three **display windows**: A command window is used to enter commands and data and to print results; a graphics window is used to display plots and graphs; and an edit window is used to create and modify M-files, which are files that contain a program or script of MATLAB commands. When you first enter MATLAB, the command window will be the active window. The edit window appears when program files are created or loaded; the graphics window appears when plots are generated. As you execute commands, appropriate windows will automatically appear. You can choose the window that you want to be active by simply clicking the mouse within it.

There are several commands for clearing windows. The `clc` command clears the command window, and the `clf` command clears the current figure and thus clears the graph window. The command `clear` does not affect the windows, but it does remove all variables from memory. In general, it is a good idea to start programs with the `clear` and `clf` commands to be sure that the memory has been cleared and that the graph window has been cleared and reset.

If you want to see some of the capabilities of MATLAB, enter the `demo` command. This initiates the MATLAB Expo, a graphical demonstration environment that illustrates some of the different types of operations that can be performed with MATLAB. If you enter the `help` command, a help menu appears.

Abort

It is important to know how to **abort** a command in MATLAB. For example, there may be times when your commands cause the computer to print seemingly endless lists of numbers or when the computer seems to go into an endless loop. In these cases, hold down the control key and press c to generate a local abort within MATLAB. The control-c sequence is sometimes written as ^c. However, this can be confusing because the sequence does not include the ^ character.

2.2   Scalars, Vectors, and Matrices

When solving engineering problems, it is important to be able to visualize the data related to the problem. Sometimes the data is just a single number, such as the radius of a circle. Other times the data may be a coordinate on a plane that can be represented as a pair of numbers, with one number representing the x coordinate and the other number representing the y coordinate. In another problem we might have a set of four x-y-z coordinates that represent the four vertices of a pyramid with a triangular base in a 3-dimensional space. We can represent all these examples using a special type of data structure called a **matrix**. A matrix is a set of numbers arranged in a rectangular grid of rows and columns. Thus, a single point can be considered a matrix with one row and one column, an x-y coordinate can be considered a matrix with one row and two columns, and a set of four x-y-z coordinates can be considered a matrix with four rows and three columns. Examples are:

Matrix

$$A = [\, 3.5\,] \qquad B = [\, 1.5 \quad 3.1\,]$$

$$C = \begin{bmatrix} -1 & 0 & 0 \\ 1 & 1 & 0 \\ 1 & -1 & 0 \\ 0 & 0 & 2 \end{bmatrix}$$

Note that the data within a matrix are written within brackets. When a matrix has one row and one column, we can also refer to the number as a scalar. Similarly, when a matrix has one row or one column, we can refer to it as a row vector or a column vector.

When we use a matrix, we need a way to refer to individual elements or numbers in the matrix. A simple method for specifying an element in the matrix uses the row and column number. For example, if we refer to the value in row 4 and column 3 in the matrix C in the previous example, there is no ambiguity— we are referring to the value 2. We use the row and column number as **Subscripts** **subscripts**; thus, $C_{4,3}$ is equal to 2. To refer to the entire matrix, we use the name without subscripts, as in C, or we use brackets around an individual element reference that uses letters instead of numbers for the subscripts, as in $[C_{i,j}]$. In formal mathematical notation, the matrix name is usually an uppercase letter, with the subscripted references using a lowercase letter, as in C, $c_{4,3}$ and $[c_{i,j}]$. However, because MATLAB is case sensitive, C and c represent different matrices. Therefore, in your MATLAB programs, you will need to consistently use uppercase and lowercase letters in references to a specific matrix.

The size of a matrix is specified by the number of rows and columns. Thus, using our previous example, C is a matrix with four rows and three columns, or a 4×3 matrix. If a matrix contains m rows and n columns, then the number of values is the product of m and n; thus, C contains 12 values. If a matrix has the same **Square matrix** number of rows as columns, it is called a **square matrix**.

Practice!

Answer the following questions about this matrix:

$$G = \begin{bmatrix} 0.6 & 1.5 & 2.3 & -0.5 \\ 8.2 & 0.5 & -0.1 & -2.0 \\ 5.7 & 8.2 & 9 & 1.5 \\ 0.5 & 0.5 & 2.4 & 0.5 \\ 1.2 & -2.3 & -4.5 & 0.5 \end{bmatrix}$$

1. What is the size of G?
2. Give the subscript references for all locations that contain the value 0.5.

In MATLAB programs, we assign names to the scalars, vectors, and matrices that we use. The following rules apply to these variable names:

- Variable names must start with a letter.
- Variable names can contain letters, digits, and the underscore character (_).

- Variable names can be of any length, but they must be unique within the first 19 characters.

Because MATLAB is case sensitive, the names Time, TIME, and time all represent different variables.

INITIALIZING VARIABLES

We present four methods for initializing matrices in MATLAB. The first method explicitly lists the values, the second reads the data from a data file, the third uses the colon operator, and the fourth reads data from the keyboard.

Explicit Lists. The simplest way to define a matrix is to use a list of numbers, as shown in the following example, which define the matrices **A**, **B**, and **C** that we used in our previous example:

```
A = [3.5];
B = [1.5,3.1];
C = [-1,0,0; 1,1,0; 1,-1,0; 0,0,2];
```

These statements are examples of the assignment statement, which consists of a variable name followed by an equal sign and the data values to assign to the variable. The data values are enclosed in brackets in row order. Semicolons separate the rows, and the values in the rows can be separated by commas or blanks. A value can contain a plus or minus sign and a decimal point, but it cannot contain a comma, as in 32,010.

When we define a matrix, MATLAB will also print the value of the matrix on the screen unless we suppress the printing with a semicolon after the definition. In our examples, we will generally include the semicolon to **suppress printing**. However, when you are first learning to define matrices, it is helpful to see the matrix values. Therefore, you may want to omit the semicolon after a matrix definition until you are confident that you know how to properly define matrices. The **who** and **whos** commands are also very helpful as you use MATLAB. The **who** command lists the matrices that you have defined, and the **whos** command lists the matrices and their sizes.

A matrix can also be defined by listing each row on a separate line, as in the following set of MATLAB commands:

```
C = [-1,   0,   0
      1,   1,   0
      1,  -1,   0
      0,   0,   2];
```

Suppress printing

If there are too many numbers in a row of the matrix to fit on one line, you can continue the statement on the next line, but a comma and three periods (an **ellipsis**)

Ellipsis

are needed at the end of the line to indicate that the row is to be continued. For example, if we want to define a row vector **F** with ten values, we could use either of the following statements:

```
F = [1,52,64,197,42,-42,55,82,22,109];
F = [1, 52, 64, 197, 42, -42, . . .
     55, 82, 22, 109];
```

MATLAB also allows you to define a matrix using another matrix that has already been defined. For example, consider the following statements:

```
B = [1.5, 3.1];
S = [3.0 B];
```

These commands are equivalent to the following:

```
S = [3.0 1.5 3.1];
```

We can also change values in a matrix or add additional values using a reference to specific locations. Thus, the following command

```
S(2) = -1.0;
```

changes the second value in the matrix **s** from 1.5 to -1.0.

You can also extend a matrix by defining new elements. If we execute the following command,

```
S(4) = 5.5;
```

the matrix **s** will have four values instead of three. If we execute the following command,

```
S(8) = 9.5;
```

then the matrix **s** will have eight values, and the values of **s(5)**, **s(6)**, and **s(7)** are automatically set to zero because no values were given for them.

Practice!

Give the sizes of these matrices. Then check your answers by entering the commands in MATLAB. In these problems, a matrix definition may refer to a previously defined matrix.

1. **B = [2; 4; 6; 10]**
2. **C = [5 3 5; 6 2 -3]**

3.   E = [3 5 10 0; 0 0 . . . .
            0 3; 3 9 9 8]

4.   T = [4 24 9]

      Q = [T 0 T]

5.   V = [C(2,1); B]

6.   A(2,1) = -3

Data Files. Matrices can also be defined from information that has been stored in a data file. Matlab can interface to two different types of data files—MAT-files and ASCII files. A MAT-file contains data stored in a memory-efficient binary format, whereas an ASCII file contains information stored in ASCII characters. MAT-files are preferable for data that is going to be generated and used by Matlab programs. ASCII files are necessary if the data is to be shared (imported or exported) to programs other than Matlab programs.

MAT-files

MAT-files are generated by a MATLAB program using the **save** command, which contains a file name and the matrices to be stored in the file. The **.mat** extension is automatically added to the filename. For example, the following command

        save data_1 x y;

will save the matrices **x** and **y** in a file named **data_1.mat**. To restore these matrices in a MATLAB program, use the command

        load data_1;

ASCII data file

An **ASCII data file** that is going to be used with a MATLAB program should contain only numeric information, and each row of the file should contain the same number of data values. The file can be generated using a word processor program or an editor. It can also be generated by running a program written in a computer language, such as a C program, or it can be generated by a MATLAB program using the following form of the **save** command:

        save data_2.dat z /ascii;

This command causes each row of the matrix **z** to be written to a separate line in the data file. The **.mat** extension is not added to an ASCII file. However, as we illustrated in this example, we recommend that ASCII filenames include the extension **.dat** so that it is easy to distinguish them from MAT-files and M-files.

Suppose that an ASCII file named **data_3.dat** contains a set of values that represent the time and corresponding distance of a runner from the starting line in a race. Each time and its corresponding distance value are on a separate line of the data file. Thus, the first few lines in the data file might have the following form:

```
0.0     0.0
0.1     3.5
0.2     6.8
```

The **load** command followed by the filename will read the information into a matrix with the same name as the data file. For example, consider this statement:

```
load data_3.dat;
```

The data values will automatically be stored in the matrix **data_3**, which has two columns.

Colon Operator. The colon operator is a very powerful operator for creating new matrices. For example, the colon operator can be used to create vectors from a matrix. When a colon is used in a matrix reference in place of a specific subscript, the colon represents the entire row or column. For example, using the **data_3** matrix that was read from a data file in the previous discussion, the following commands will store the first column of **data_3** in the column vector **x** and the second column of **data_3** in the column vector **y**:

```
x = data_3(:,1);
y = data_3(:,2);
```

The colon operator can also be used to generate new matrices. If a colon is used to separate two integers, the colon operator generates all the integers between the two specified integers. For example, the following notation generates a vector named **H** that contains the numbers from 1 to 8:

```
H = 1:8;
```

If colons are used to separate three numbers, then the colon operator generates values between the first and third numbers, using the second number as the increment. For example, the following notation generates a row vector named **time** that contains the numbers from 0.0 to 5.0 in increments of 0.5:

```
time = 0.0:0.5:5.0;
```

The increment can also be negative, as shown in the following example, which generates the numbers 10, 9, 8, . . . 0 in the row vector named **values**:

```
values = 10:-1:0;
```

Submatrix

The colon operator can also be used to select a **submatrix** from another matrix. For example, assume that **c** is the following matrix:

$$C = \begin{bmatrix} -1 & 0 & 0 \\ 1 & 1 & 0 \\ 1 & -1 & 0 \\ 0 & 0 & 2 \end{bmatrix}$$

If we then execute the following commands

```
C_partial_1 = C(:,2:3);
C_partial_2 = C(3:4,1:2);
```

we have defined the following matrices:

$$C\_partial\_1 = \begin{bmatrix} 0 & 0 \\ 1 & 0 \\ -1 & 0 \\ 0 & 2 \end{bmatrix} \qquad C\_partial\_2 = \begin{bmatrix} 1 & -1 \\ 0 & 0 \end{bmatrix}$$

If the colon notation defines a matrix with invalid subscripts, as in `c(5:6,:)`, an error message is displayed.

Empty matrix

In MATLAB it is valid to have a matrix that is empty. For example, the following statements will each generate an **empty matrix**:

```
a = [];
b = 4:-1:5;
```

Note that an empty matrix is different from a matrix that contains only zeros.

The use of the expression `c(:)` is equivalent to one long column matrix that contains the first column of **c**, followed by the second column of **c**, and so on.

Transpose

An operator that is very useful with matrices is the **transpose** operator. The transpose of a matrix **a** is denoted by **a'** and represents a new matrix in which the rows of **a** are transformed into the columns of **a'**. In Chapter 4, we discuss this operator in more detail, but for now we will use the transpose operator only to turn a row vector into a column vector and a column vector into a row vector. This characteristic can be very useful when printing vectors. For example, suppose that we generate two vectors, **x** and **y**. We then want to print the values such that `x(1)` and `y(1)` are on the same line, `x(2)` and `y(2)` are on the same line, and so on. A simple way to do this is

```
x = 0:4;
y = 5:5:25;
[x' y']
```

The output generated by these statements is

```
0 5
1 10
2 15
3 20
4 25
```

This operator will also be useful in generating some of the tables specified in the problems at the end of this chapter.

Practice!

Give the contents of the following matrices. Then check your answers by entering the MATLAB commands. Use the following matrix **G**:

$$G = \begin{bmatrix} 0.6 & 1.5 & 2.3 & -0.5 \\ 8.2 & 0.5 & -0.1 & -2.0 \\ 5.7 & 8.2 & 9.0 & 1.5 \\ 0.5 & 0.5 & 2.4 & 0.5 \\ 1.2 & -2.3 & -4.5 & 0.5 \end{bmatrix}$$

1. `A = G(:,2)`
2. `C = 10:15`
3. `D = [4:9; 1:6]`
4. `F = 0.0:0.1:1.0`
5. `T1 = G(4:5,1:3)`
6. `T2 = G(1:2:5,:)`

User Input. The values for a matrix can also be entered through the keyboard using the **input** command, which displays a text string and then waits for input. The value entered by the user is then stored in the variable specified. If more than one value is to be entered by the user, they must be enclosed in brackets. If the user strikes the return key without entering input values, an empty matrix is returned. If the command does not end with a semicolon, the values entered for the matrix are printed.

Consider the following command:

```
z = input('Enter values for z in brackets:');
```

When this command is executed, the text string **Enter values for z in brackets** is displayed on the terminal screen. The user can then enter an expression such as **[5.1 6.3 -18.0]**, which then specifies values for **z**. Because this **input** command ends with a semicolon, the values of **z** are not printed when the command is completed.

PRINTING MATRICES

There are several ways to print the contents of a matrix. The simplest way is to enter the name of the matrix. The name of the matrix will be repeated, and the values of the matrix will be printed starting with the next line. There are also several commands that can be used to print matrices with more control over the form of the output.

Default format

Display Format. When elements of a matrix are printed, integers are always printed as integers. Values with decimal fractions are printed using a **default format** (called a short format) that shows four decimal digits. MATLAB allows you to specify other formats (see Table 2.1) that show more significant digits. For example, to specify that we want values to be displayed in a decimal format with 14 decimal digits, we use the command `format long`. The format can be returned to a decimal format with four decimal digits using the command `format short`. Two decimal digits are displayed when the format is specified with `format bank`.

Scientific notation

When a value is very large or very small, decimal notation does not work satisfactorily. For example, a value that is used frequently in chemistry is Avogadro's constant, whose value to four significant places is 602,300,000,000,000,000,000,000. Obviously, we need a more manageable notation for very large values like Avogadro's constant or for very small values like 0.0000000031. **Scientific notation** expresses a value as a number between 1 and 10 multiplied by a power of l0. In scientific notation, Avogadro's constant becomes 6.023×10^{23}. This form is also referred to as a mantissa (6.023) and an exponent (23). In MATLAB, values in scientific notation are printed with the letter e to separate the mantissa and the exponent, as in 6.023e+23. If we want MATLAB to print values in scientific notation with five significant digits, we use the command `format short e`. To specify scientific notation with 16 significant digits, we use the command `format long e`. We can also enter values in a matrix using scientific notation, but it is important to omit blanks between the mantissa and the exponent because MATLAB will interpret 6.023e+23 as two values (6.023 and e+23), whereas 6.023e+23 will be interpreted as one value.

Another format command is `format +`. When a matrix is printed with this value, the only characters printed are plus and minus signs. If a value is positive, a plus sign will be printed; if a value is zero, a space will be skipped; if a value is negative, a negative sign will be printed. This format allows us to view a large matrix in terms of its signs. Otherwise, we would not be able to see it easily because there might be too many values in a row to fit on a single line.

For long and short formats, a common scale factor is applied to the entire matrix if the elements become very large. This scale factor is printed along with the scaled values.

Finally, the command `format compact` suppresses many of the line feeds that appear between matrix displays and allows more lines of information to be seen together on the screen. In our example output, we will assume that this command has been executed. The command `format loose` will return to the less compact display mode.

TABLE 2.1 Numeric Display Formats

MATLAB Command	Display	Example
format short	default	15.2345
format long	14 decimals	15.23453333333333
format short e	4 decimals	1.5235e + 01
format long e	15 decimals	1.523453333333333e + 01
format bank	2 decimals	15.23
format +	+ , − , blank	+

Printing Text or Matrices. The `disp` command can be used to display text enclosed in single quote marks. It can also be used to print the contents of a matrix without printing the matrix name. Thus, if a scalar `temp` contained a temperature value in degrees Fahrenheit, we could print the value on one line plus the units on the next line using these commands:

```
disp(temp); disp('degrees F')
```

If the value of temp is 78, then the output will be the following:

```
78
degrees F
```

Note that the two `disp` commands were entered on the same line so that they would be executed together.

Formatted Output. The `fprintf` command gives you even more control over the output than you have with the `disp` command. In addition to printing both text and matrix values, you can specify the format to be used in printing the values, and you can specify a skip to a new line. The general form of this command is the following:

```
fprintf(format,matrices)
```

Specifiers

The format contains the text and format specifications to be printed and is followed by the names of the matrices to be printed. Within the format, the **specifiers** `%e`, `%f`, and `%g` are used to show where the matrix values are printed. If `%e` is used, the values will be printed in an exponential notation; if `%f` is used, the values will be printed in a fixed point or decimal notation; if `%g` is used, the values will use either `%e` or `%f`, depending on which is shorter. If the string `\n` appears in the format, the line specified up to that point is printed, and the rest of the information will be printed on the next line. A format usually ends with `\n`.

A simple example of the `fprintf` command is

```
fprintf('The temperature is %f degrees F \n',temp)
```

The corresponding output is

```
The temperature is 78.000000 degrees F
```

If we modify the command to this form,

```
fprintf('The temperature is \n %f degrees F \n',temp)
```

then the output is

```
The temperature is
78.000000 degrees F
```

The format specifiers `%f`, `%e`, and `%g` can also contain information to specify the number of decimal places to print and the number of positions to allot for the corresponding value. Consider this command:

```
fprintf('The temperature is %4.1f degrees F \n',temp)
```

The value of `temp` is printed using four positions, one of which is a decimal position:

```
The temperature is 78.0 degrees F
```

The `fprintf` statement allows you to have a great deal of control over the form of the output. We will use it frequently in our examples to help you become familiar with it.

XY PLOTS

In this section we show you how to generate a simple *xy* plot from data stored in two vectors. Assume that we want to plot the following data collected from an experiment with a remotely controlled model car. The experiment is repeated ten times, and we have measured the distance that the car travels for each trial.

Trial	Distance, ft
1	58.5
2	63.8
3	64.2
4	67.3
5	71.5
6	88.3
7	90.1
8	90.6
9	89.5
10	90.4

Assume that the time values are stored in a vector called **x** and that the distance values are stored in a vector called **y**. To plot these points, we use the **plot** command, with **x** and **y** as arguments.

```
plot(x,y)
```

The plot in Figure 2.1 is automatically generated. (Slight variations in the scaling of the plot may occur because of the computer type and the size of the graphics window.)

Good engineering practice requires that we include units and a title. Therefore, we include the following commands that add a title, x and y labels, and a background grid:

```
plot(x,y),title('Laboratory Experiment 1'),
xlabel('Trial'),ylabel('Distance, ft'),grid
```

These commands generate the plot in Figure 2.2.

If you display a plot and then continue with more computations, MATLAB will generate and display the graph in the graphics window and then return immediately to execute the rest of the commands in the program. Because the plot window is replaced by the command window when MATLAB returns to finish the

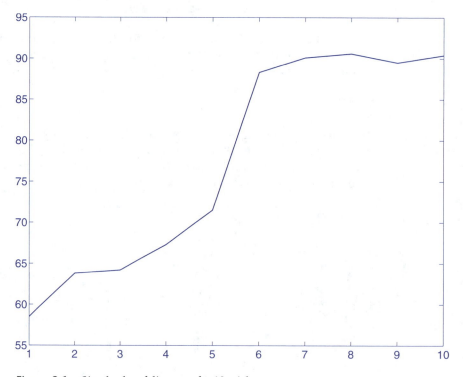

Figure 2.1   *Simple plot of distances for 10 trials.*

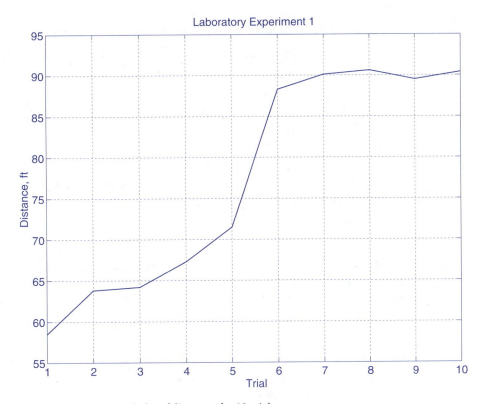

Figure 2.2   *Enhanced plot of distances for 10 trials.*

computations, you may want to use the **pause** command to halt the program temporarily to give you a chance to study the plot. Execution will continue when any key is pressed. If you want to pause for a specified number of seconds, use the **pause(n)** command, which will pause for **n** seconds before continuing. The **print** command will print the contents of the graphics window on the printer attached to the computer.

2.3   Scalar and Array Operations

Arithmetic computations are specified by matrices and constants combined with arithmetic operations. In this section, we first discuss operations involving only scalars; then we extend the operations to include element-by-element operations.

SCALAR OPERATIONS

The arithmetic operations between two scalars are shown in Table 2.2. Expressions containing scalars and scalar operations can be evaluated and stored in a

TABLE 2.2 Arithmetic Operations between Two Scalars

Operation	Algebraic Form	MATLAB
addition	$a + b$	a + b
subtraction	$a - b$	a - b
multiplication	$a \times b$	a*b
division	$\frac{a}{b}$	a/b
exponentiation	a^b	a^b

specified variable, as in the following statement, which specifies that the values in **a** and **b** are to be added and the sum stored in **x**:

```
x = a + b;
```

This assignment statement should be interpreted as specifying that the value in **a** is added to the value in **b**, and the sum is stored in **x**. If we interpret assignment statements in this way, we are not disturbed by the following valid MATLAB statement:

```
count = count + 1;
```

Clearly this statement is not a valid algebraic statement, but in MATLAB it specifies that 1 is to be added to the value in **count**, and the result stored back in **count**. Therefore, it is equivalent to specifying that the value in **count** should be incremented by 1.

It is important to recognize that a variable can store only one value at a time. For example, suppose that the following MATLAB statements were executed one after another:

```
time = 0.0;
time = 5.0;
```

The value 0.0 is stored in the variable **time** when the first statement is executed, and is then replaced by the value 5.0 when the second statement is executed.

When you enter an expression without specifying a variable to store the result, the result or answer is automatically stored in a variable named **ans**. Each time that a new value is stored in **ans**, the previous value is lost.

PRECEDENCE OF ARITHMETIC OPERATIONS

Because several operations can be combined in a single arithmetic expression, it is important to know the order in which operations are performed. Table 2.3 contains the precedence of arithmetic operations in MATLAB. Note that this precedence also follows the standard algebraic precedence.

TABLE 2.3 Precedence of Arithmetic Operations

Precedence	Operation
1	parentheses, innermost first
2	exponentiation, left to right
3	multiplication and division, left to right
4	addition and subtraction, left to right

Assume that we want to compute the area of a trapezoid, and the variable **base** contains the length of the base and that **height_1** and **height_2** contain the two heights. The area of a trapezoid can be computed using the following MATLAB statement:

```
area = 0.5*base*(height_1 + height_2);
```

Suppose that we omit the parentheses in the expression:

```
area = 0.5*base*height_1 + height_2;
```

This statement would be executed as if it were this statement:

```
area = (0.5*base*height_1) + height_2;
```

Note that although the incorrect answer has been computed, there are no error messages printed to alert us to the error. Therefore, it is important to be very careful when converting equations into MATLAB statements. Adding extra parentheses is an easy way to be sure that computations are done in the order that you want.

If an expression is long, break it into multiple statements. For example, consider the following equation:

$$f = \frac{x^3 - 2x^2 + x - 6.3}{x^2 + 0.05005x - 3.14}$$

The value of **f** could be computed using the following MATLAB statements:

```
numerator = x^3 - 2*x^2 + x - 6.3;
denominator = x^2 + 0.05005*x - 3.14;
f = numerator/denominator;
```

It is better to use several statements that are easy to understand than to use one statement that requires careful thought to figure out the order of operations.

Practice!

Give MATLAB commands to compute the following values. Assume that the variables in the equations are scalars and that they have been assigned values.

1.   Correction factor in pressure calculation:

$$\text{factor} = 1 + \frac{b}{v} + \frac{c}{v^2}$$

2.   Slope between two points:

$$\text{slope} = \frac{y_2 - y_1}{x_2 - x_1}$$

3.   Resistance of a parallel circuit:

$$\text{resistance} = \frac{1}{\dfrac{1}{r_1} + \dfrac{1}{r_2} + \dfrac{1}{r_3}}$$

4.   Pressure loss from pipe friction:

$$\text{loss} = f \cdot p \cdot \frac{1}{d} \cdot \frac{v^2}{2}$$

COMPUTATIONAL LIMITATIONS

The variables stored in a computer have a wide range of values that they can assume. For most computers, the range of values extends from 10^{-308} to 10^{308}, which should be enough to accommodate most computations. However, it is possible for the result of an expression to be outside of this range. For example, suppose that we execute the following commands:

```
x = 2.5e200;
y = 1.0e200;
z = x*y;
```

Overflow

If we assume the range of values is from 10^{-308} to 10^{308}, then the values of **x** and **y** are within the allowable range. However, the value of **z** is 2.5e400, and this value exceeds the range. This error is called exponent **overflow** because the exponent of the result of an arithmetic operation is too large to store in the computer's memory. In MATLAB, the result of an exponent overflow is ∞.

Underflow

Exponent **underflow** is a similar error, caused by the exponent of the result of an arithmetic operation being too small to store in the computer's memory. Using the same allowable range, we obtain an exponent underflow with the following commands:

```
x = 2.5e-200;
y = 1.0e200;
z = x/y;
```

Again, the values of **x** and **y** are within the allowable range, but the value of **z** should be 2.5e−400. Because the exponent is less than the minimum, we have caused an exponent underflow error to occur. In MATLAB, the result of an exponent underflow is zero.

Division by zero

We know that **division by zero** is an invalid operation. If an expression results in a division by zero in MATLAB, the result of the division is ∞. MATLAB will print a warning message, and subsequent computations continue.

ARRAY OPERATIONS

Array operation

An **array operation** is performed element-by-element. For example, suppose that **A** is a row vector with five elements, and **B** is a row vector with five elements. One way to generate a new row vector **c** with values that are the products of corresponding values in **A** and **B** is the following:

```
C(1) = A(1)*B(1);
C(2) = A(2)*B(2);
C(3) = A(3)*B(3);
C(4) = A(4)*B(4);
C(5) = A(5)*B(5);
```

These commands are essentially scalar commands because each command multiplies a single value by another single value and stores the product in a third value. To indicate that we want to perform an element-by-element multiplication between two matrices of the same size, we use an asterisk preceded by a period. Thus, the five statements above can be replaced by the following:

```
C = A.*B;
```

Omitting the period before the asterisk is a serious omission because the statement then specifies a matrix operation, not an element-by-element operation. Matrix operations are discussed in Chapter 4.

For addition and subtraction, array operations and matrix operations are the same, so we do not need to distinguish between them. However, array operations for multiplication, division, and exponentiation are different from matrix operations for multiplication, division, and exponentiation, so we need to include a period to specify an array operation. These rules are summarized in Table 2.4.

TABLE 2.4 Element-by-Element Operations

Operation	Algebraic Form	MATLAB
addition	$a + b$	`a + b`
subtraction	$a - b$	`a - b`
multiplication	$a \times b$	`a.*b`
division	$\dfrac{a}{b}$	`a./b`
exponentiation	a^b	`a.^b`

Element-by-element operations, or array operations, apply not only to operations between two matrices of the same size, but also to operations between a scalar and nonscalar. However, multiplication of a matrix by a scalar can be written either way. Thus, the two statements in each set of statements below are equivalent for a matrix **A**:

```
B = 3*A;
B = 3.*A;

C = A/5;
C = A./5;
```

The resulting matrices **B** and **C** will be the same size as **A**.

To illustrate the array operations for vectors, consider the following two row vectors:

A = [2 5 6]   B = [2 3 5]

If we compute the array product of **A** and **B** using the following statement,

```
C = A. *B;
```

then **C** will contain the following values:

C = [4 15 30]

The array division command

```
C = A./B;
```

will generate a new vector in which each element of **A** is divided by the corresponding element of **B**. Thus, **C** will contain the following values

C = [1 1.6667 1.2]

Array exponentiation is also an element-wise operation. For example, consider the following statement:

```
A = [2, 5, 6];
B = [2, 3, 5];
C = A.^2;
D = A.^B;
```

The vectors **C** and **D** are the following;

C = [4 25 36]   D = [4 125 7776]

We can also use a scalar base to a vector exponent, as in

```
C = 3.0.^A;
```

which generates a vector with the following values:

C = [9 243 729]

This vector could also have been computed with the statement

```
C = (3).^A;
```

If you are not sure that you have written the correct expression, always test it with simple examples like the ones we have used.

The previous examples used vectors, but the same rules apply to matrices with rows and columns, as shown by the following statements:

```
d = [1:5; -1:-1:-5];
p = d.*5;
q = d.^3;
```

The values of these matrices are shown below:

$$d = \begin{bmatrix} 1 & 2 & 3 & 4 & 5 \\ -1 & -2 & -3 & -4 & -5 \end{bmatrix}$$

$$p = \begin{bmatrix} 5 & 10 & 15 & 20 & 25 \\ -5 & -10 & -15 & -20 & -25 \end{bmatrix}$$

$$q = \begin{bmatrix} 1 & 8 & 27 & 64 & 125 \\ -1 & -8 & -27 & -64 & -125 \end{bmatrix}$$

Practice!

Give the values in the vector c after executing the following statements, where A and B contain the values shown. Check your answers using MATLAB.

A = [2 −1 5 0]   B = [3 2 −1 4]

1.   `C = B + A - 3;`
2.   `C = 2*A + A.^B;`
3.   `C = A./B;`
4.   `C = A.^B;`
5.   `C = 2.^B + A;`
6.   `C = 2*B/3.*A;`

2.4   Special Values and Special Matrices

MATLAB includes a number of predefined constants, special values, and special matrices that are available to our programs. Most of these special values and special matrices are generated by MATLAB using functions. A MATLAB function typically uses inputs called **arguments** to compute a matrix, although some functions do not require any input arguments. In this section, we give some examples of MATLAB functions, and in Chapter 3 we review a large number of additional MATLAB functions.

Arguments

SPECIAL VALUES

The scalar values that are available to use in MATLAB programs are described in the following list:

pi	Represents π.
i, j	Represents $\sqrt{-1}$.
Inf	Represents infinity, which typically occurs as a result of a division by zero. A warning message will be printed when this value is computed; if you display a matrix containing this value, the value will print as ∞.
NaN	Represents Not-a-Number and typically occurs when an expression is undefined, as in the division of zero by zero.
clock	Represents the current time in a six-element row vector containing year, month, day, hour, minute, and seconds.
date	Represents the current date in a character string format, such as **20-Jun-96**.
eps	Represents the floating-point precision for the computer being used. This epsilon precision is the smallest amount with which two values can differ in the computer.
ans	Represents a value computed by an expression that is computed but not stored in a variable name.

SPECIAL MATRICES

MATLAB contains a group of functions that generate special matrices; we present some of these function here.

Matrix of Zeros. The **zeros** function generates a matrix containing all zeros. If the argument to the function is a scalar, as in **zeros(6)**, the function will generate a square matrix using the argument as both the number of rows and the number of columns. If the function has two scalar arguments, as in **zeros(m,n)**, the function will generate a matrix with **m** rows and **n** columns. Because the **size** function returns two scalar arguments that represent the number of rows and the number of columns in a matrix, we can use the **size** function to generate a matrix of zeros that is the same size as another matrix. The following statements illustrate these various cases:

```
A = zeros(3);
B = zeros(3,2);
C = [ 1 2 3 ; 4 2 5];
D = zeros(size(C));
```

The matrices generated are the following:

$$A = \begin{bmatrix} 0 & 0 & 0 \\ 0 & 0 & 0 \\ 0 & 0 & 0 \end{bmatrix} \quad B = \begin{bmatrix} 0 & 0 \\ 0 & 0 \\ 0 & 0 \end{bmatrix}$$

$$C = \begin{bmatrix} 1 & 2 & 3 \\ 4 & 2 & 5 \end{bmatrix} \quad D = \begin{bmatrix} 0 & 0 & 0 \\ 0 & 0 & 0 \end{bmatrix}$$

Matrix of Ones. The **ones** function generates a matrix containing all ones, just as the **zeros** function generates a matrix containing all zeros. If the argument to the function is a scalar, as in **ones(6)**, the function will generate a square matrix using the argument as both the number of rows and the number of columns. If the function has two scalar arguments, as in **ones(m,n)**, the function will generate a matrix with **m** rows and **n** columns. To generate a matrix of zeros that is the same size as another matrix, use the **size** function to determine the correct number of rows and columns. The following statements illustrate these various cases:

```
A = ones(3);
B = ones(3,2);
C = [ 1 2 3 ; 4 2 5];
D = ones(size(C));
```

The matrices generated are the following:

$$A = \begin{bmatrix} 1 & 1 & 1 \\ 1 & 1 & 1 \\ 1 & 1 & 1 \end{bmatrix} \quad B = \begin{bmatrix} 1 & 1 \\ 1 & 1 \\ 1 & 1 \end{bmatrix}$$

$$C = \begin{bmatrix} 1 & 2 & 3 \\ 4 & 2 & 5 \end{bmatrix} \quad D = \begin{bmatrix} 1 & 1 & 1 \\ 1 & 1 & 1 \end{bmatrix}$$

Identity Matrix. An identity matrix is a matrix with ones on the main diagonal and zeros elsewhere. For example, the following matrix is an identity matrix with four rows and four columns:

$$\begin{bmatrix} 1 & 0 & 0 & 0 \\ 0 & 1 & 0 & 0 \\ 0 & 0 & 1 & 0 \\ 0 & 0 & 0 & 1 \end{bmatrix}$$

Main diagonal   Note that the **main diagonal** is the diagonal containing elements in which the row number is the same as the column number. Therefore, the subscripts for elements on the main diagonal are (1,1), (2,2), (3,3), and so on.

In MATLAB, identity matrices can be generated using the **eye** function. The arguments of the **eye** function are similar to those for the **zeros** function and the **ones** function. If the function has one scalar argument, as in **eye(6)**, the function will generate an identity matrix using the argument as both the number of rows and the number of columns. If the function has two scalar arguments, as in **eye(m,n)**, the function will generate an identity matrix with **m** rows and **n** columns. To generate an identity matrix that is the same size as another matrix, use the **size** function to determine the correct number of rows and columns. Although most applications use a square identity matrix, the definition can be extended to non-square matrices. The following statements illustrate these various cases:

```
A = eye(3);
B = eye(3,2);
C = [ 1 2 3 ; 4 2 5];
D = eye(size(C));
```

The matrices generated are the following:

$$A = \begin{bmatrix} 1 & 0 & 0 \\ 0 & 1 & 0 \\ 0 & 0 & 1 \end{bmatrix} \qquad B = \begin{bmatrix} 1 & 0 \\ 0 & 1 \\ 0 & 0 \end{bmatrix}$$

$$C = \begin{bmatrix} 1 & 2 & 3 \\ 4 & 2 & 5 \end{bmatrix} \qquad D = \begin{bmatrix} 1 & 0 & 0 \\ 0 & 1 & 0 \end{bmatrix}$$

We recommend that you do not name an identity matrix **i** because **i** will not represent $\sqrt{-1}$ in statements that follow.

2.5   Additional Plotting Capabilities

The most common plot used by engineers and scientists is the xy plot. The data that we plot are usually read from a data file or computed in our programs and stored in vectors that we will call x and y. We generally assume that the x values **Independent** represent the **independent variable** and that the y values represent the depen-
variable dent variable. The y values can be computed as a function of x, or the x and y values might be measured in an experiment. We now present some additional ways of displaying this information.

PLOT COMMANDS

Most plots that we generate assume that the x and y axes are divided into **Logarithmic** equally spaced intervals; these plots are called linear plots. Occasionally, we
scale may like to use a **logarithmic scale** on one or both of the axes. A logarithmic

scale (base 10) is convenient when a variable ranges over many orders of magnitude because the wide range of values can be graphed without compressing the smaller values.

The MATLAB commands for generating linear and logarithmic plots of the vectors **x** and **y** are the following:

`plot(x,y)`	Generates a linear plot of the values of **x** and **y**.
`semilogx(x,y)`	Generates a plot of the values of **x** and **y** using a logarithmic scale for **x** and a linear scale for **y**.
`semilogy(x,y)`	Generates a plot of the values of **x** and **y** using a linear scale for **x** and a logarithmic scale for **y**.
`loglog(x,y)`	Generates a plot of the values of **x** and **y** using logarithmic scales for both **x** and **y**.

It is important to recognize that the logarithm of a negative value or of zero does not exist. Therefore, if the data to be plotted in a semilog plot or log-log plot contain negative values or zeros, a warning message will be printed by MATLAB informing you that these data points have been omitted from the data plotted.

Each of these commands can also be executed with one argument, as in `plot(y)`. In these cases, the plots are generated with the values of the indices of the vector **y** used as the **x** values.

MULTIPLE PLOTS

A simple way to plot multiple curves on the same graph is to use multiple arguments in a plot command, as in

`plot(x,y,w,z)`

where the variables **x**, **y**, **w**, and **z** are vectors. When this command is executed, the curve corresponding to **x** versus **y** will be plotted, and then the curve corresponding to **w** versus **z** will be plotted on the same graph. The advantage of this technique is that the number of points in the two plots do not have to be the same. MATLAB will automatically select different line types so that you can distinguish between the two plots.

LINE AND MARK STYLE

The command `plot(x,y)` generates a line plot that connects the points represented by the vectors **x** and **y** with line segments. You can also select other line types—dashed, dotted, and dash-dot. You can also select a point plot instead of a line plot. With a point plot, the points represented by the vectors will be marked with a point instead of connected by line segments. You can also select characters other than a point to indicate the points. The other choices are plus signs, stars, circles, and *x*-marks. Table 2.5 contains these different options for lines and marks.

TABLE 2.5 Line and Mark Options			
Line Type	**Indicator**	**Point Type**	**Indicator**
solid	–	point	.
dashed	– –	plus	+
dotted	:	star	*
dash-dot	– .	circle	o
		x-mark	x

The following command illustrates the use of line and mark styles. It generates a solid line plot of the points represented by the vectors **x** and **y**, and then plots the points themselves with circles:

```
plot(x,y,x,y,'o')
```

This type of plot is shown in Figure 6.1 on page 114.

AXES SCALING

MATLAB automatically scales the axes to fit the data values. However, you can override this scaling with the **axis** command. There are several forms of the **axis** command:

axis   Freezes the current axis scaling for subsequent plots. A second execution of the command returns the system to automatic scaling.

axis(v)   Specifies axis using is a four-element vector **v** that contains the scaling values, **[xmin,xmax,ymin,ymax]**.

These commands are especially useful when you want to compare curves from different plots because it can be difficult to visually compare curves plotted with different axes. The **plot** command precedes the corresponding **axis** command.

SUBPLOTS

Subwindows

The **subplot** command allows you to split the graph window into **subwindows**. The possible splits can be to two subwindows or four subwindows. Two subwindows can be arranged as either top and bottom or left and right. A four-window split has two subwindows on the top and two subwindows on the bottom. The arguments to the **subplot** command are three integers *m*, *n*, *p*. The digits *m* and *n* specify that the graph window is to be split into an *m*-by-*n* grid of smaller windows, and the digit *p* specifies the *p*th window for the current plot. The windows are numbered from left to right, top to bottom. Therefore, the following commands specify that the graph window is to be split into a top plot and a bottom plot, and the current plot is to be placed in the top subwindow:

```
subplot(2,1,1), plot(x,y)
```

Figure 2.3 contains four plots that illustrate the **subplot** command along with the linear and logarithmic plot commands. This figure was generated using the following statements:

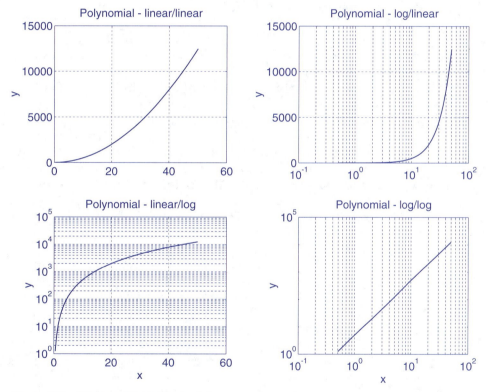

Figure 2.3   *Linear and logarithmic plots.*

```
%  Generate plots of a polynomial.
%
x = 0:0.5:50;
y = 5*x.^2;
subplot(2,2,1),plot(x,y),
    title('Polynomial - linear/linear'),
    ylabel('y'),grid,
```

```
subplot(2,2,2),semilogx(x,y),
   title('Polynomial - log/linear'),
   ylabel('y'),grid,
subplot(2,2,3),semilogy(x,y),
   title('Polynomial - linear/log'),
   xlabel('x'),ylabel('y'),grid,
subplot(2,2,4),loglog(x,y),
   title('Polynomial - log/log'),
   xlabel('x'),ylabel('y'),grid
```

Another example of the **subplot** command is included in the next section.

2.6   Problem Solving Applied: Velocity Computation

Unducted fan

In this section, we perform computations in an application related to the vehicle performance grand challenge. An advanced turboprop engine called an **unducted fan** (UDF) is one of the promising new propulsion technologies being developed for future transport aircraft. Turboprop engines, which have been in use for decades, combine the power and reliability of jet engines with the efficiency of propellers. They are a significant improvement over earlier piston-powered propeller engines. Their application has been limited to smaller commuter-type aircraft, however, because they are not as fast or powerful as the fanjet engines used on larger airliners. The UDF engine employs significant advancements in propeller technology, which narrow the performance gap between turboprops and fanjets. New materials, blade shapes, and higher rotation speeds enable UDF-powered aircraft to fly almost as fast as fanjets, and with greater fuel efficiency. The UDF is also significantly quieter than the conventional turboprop.

During a test flight of a UDF-powered aircraft, the test pilot has set the engine power level at 40,000 Newtons, which causes the 20,000-kg aircraft to attain a cruise speed of 180 m/s (meters/second). The engine throttles are then set to a power level of 60,000 Newtons, and the aircraft begins to accelerate. As the speed of the plane increases, the aerodynamic drag increases in proportion to the square of the airspeed. Eventually, the aircraft reaches a new cruise speed where the thrust from the UDF engines is just offset by the drag. The equations used to estimate the velocity and acceleration of the aircraft from the time that the throttle is reset until the plane reaches its new cruise speed (at approximately 120 s) are the following:

$$\text{velocity} = 0.00001\ \text{time}^3 - 0.00488\ \text{time}^2$$
$$+ 0.75795\ \text{time} + 181.3566$$

$$\text{acceleration} = 3 - 0.000062\ \text{velocity}^2$$

Write a MATLAB program that asks the user to enter a beginning time and an ending time (both in seconds) that define an interval of time over which we want to plot the velocity and acceleration of the aircraft. Assume that a time of zero represents the point at which the power level was increased. The ending time should be less than or equal to 120 seconds.

1.   PROBLEM STATEMENT

Compute the new velocity and acceleration of the aircraft after a change in power level.

2.   INPUT/OUTPUT DESCRIPTION

The following diagram shows that the input to the program is starting and ending times and that the output of the program is a plot of the velocity and acceleration values over this window of time.

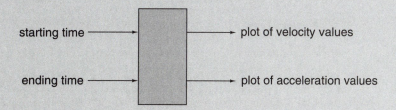

3.   HAND EXAMPLE

Because the program is generating a plot for a specified window of time, we will assume that the window is from 0 to 5 seconds. We then compute a few values with a calculator that can be compared to the values from the plot generated by the program.

Time (s)	Velocity (m/s)	Acceleration (m/s^2)
0.0	181.3566	0.9608
3.0	183.5868	0.9103
5.0	185.0256	0.8775

4.   ALGORITHM DEVELOPMENT

The generation of the plot of the velocity and acceleration values requires the following steps:

1.   Read time interval limits.

2.   Compute corresponding velocity and acceleration values.

3.   Plot new velocity and acceleration.

Because the time interval depends on the input values, it may be a very small interval or a large interval. Therefore, instead of computing velocity and acceleration values at specified points, such as every 0.1 seconds, we will compute 100 points over the specified interval.

```
% These commands generate and plot velocity and
% acceleration values in a user-specified interval.
%
start_time = input('Enter start time (in seconds): ');
end_time = input('Enter ending time (max of 120 seconds): ');
%
time_incr = (end_time - start_time)/99;
time = start_time:time_incr:end_time;
velocity = 0.00001*time.^3 - 0.00488*time.^2 . . .
           + 0.75795*time + 181.3566;
acceleration = 3 - 0.000062*velocity.^2;
%
subplot(2,1,1),plot(time,velocity),title('Velocity'),
    ylabel('meters/second'),grid,
subplot(2,1,2),plot(time,acceleration),title('Acceleration'),
    xlabel('Time, s'),ylabel('meters/second^2'),grid;
```

5.   TESTING

We first test the program using the data from the hand example. This generates the following interaction:

```
Enter start time (in seconds): 0
Enter ending time (max of 120 seconds): 5
```

The plot generated by the program is shown in Figure 2.4. Because the values computed match the hand example, we can test the program with other time values. If the values had not matched the hand example, we would need to determine if the error was in the hand example or in the program. The plot generated for the time interval from 0 to 120 seconds is shown in Figure 2.5. Note that the acceleration approaches zero as the velocity approaches its new cruise speed.

CHAPTER SUMMARY

In this chapter we have introduced you to the MATLAB environment. The primary data structure in MATLAB is a matrix, which can be a single point (a scalar), a list of values (a vector), or a rectangular grid of values with rows and columns. Values can be entered into a matrix using an explicit listing of the values. Values

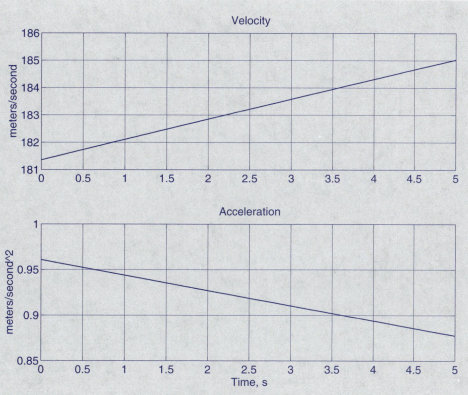

Figure 2.4 *Velocity and acceleration from 0 to 5 seconds.*

can also be loaded into a matrix from MAT-files or ASCII files. Values can also be entered into a matrix using a colon operator that allows us to specify a starting value, an increment, and an ending value for generating the sequence of values. We explored the various mathematical operations that are performed in an element-by-element manner. After a number of examples, we then demonstrated how to generate simple *xy* plots of data values. The chapter closed with an application that plotted data from an experimental aircraft engine.

MATLAB SUMMARY

This MATLAB summary lists all the special characters, commands, and functions that were defined in this chapter. A brief description is also included for each one.

SPECIAL CHARACTERS

[ ]	forms matrices
( )	forms subscripts
,	separates subscripts or matrix elements
;	separates commands or matrix rows

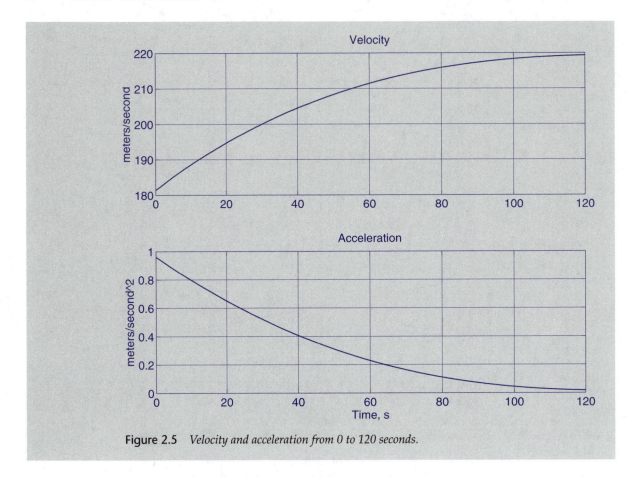

Figure 2.5   *Velocity and acceleration from 0 to 120 seconds.*

%	indicates comments
:	generates matrices
+	scalar and array addition
–	scalar and array subtraction
*	scalar multiplication
.*	array multiplication
/	scalar division
./	array division
^	scalar exponentiation
.^	array exponentiation

COMMANDS AND FUNCTIONS

ans	stores expression values
axis	controls axis scaling

`^c`	generates a local abort
`clc`	clears command screen
`clear`	clears workspace
`clf`	clears figure
`clock`	represents the current time
`date`	represents the current date
`demo`	runs demonstrations
`disp`	displays matrix or text
`eps`	represents floating-point precision
`eye`	generates identity matrix
`exit`	terminates MATLAB
`format +`	sets format to plus and minus signs only
`format compact`	sets format to compact form
`format long`	sets format to long decimal
`format long e`	sets format to long exponential
`format loose`	sets format to noncompact form
`format short`	sets format to short decimal
`format short e`	sets format to short exponential
`fprintf`	prints formatted information
`grid`	inserts grid in a plot
`help`	invokes help facility
`i`	represents the value $\sqrt{-1}$
`Inf`	represents the value ∞
`input`	accepts input from the keyboard
`j`	represents the value $\sqrt{-1}$
`load`	loads matrices from a file
`loglog`	generates a log-log plot
`NaN`	represents the value Not-a-Number
`ones`	generates matrix of ones
`pause`	temporarily halts a program
`pi`	represents the value π
`plot`	generates a linear xy plot
`print`	prints the graphics window
`quit`	terminates MATLAB
`save`	saves variables in a file
`semilogx`	generates a log-linear plot
`semilogy`	generates a linear-log plot
`size`	determines row and column dimensions
`subplot`	splits graphics window into subwindows
`title`	adds a title to a plot

who	lists variables in memory
whos	lists variables and their sizes
xlabel	adds x axis label to a plot
ylabel	adds y axis label to a plot
zeros	generates matrix of zeros

PROBLEMS

In Problems 1–10, print the specified tables using the transpose operator as needed. Include a table heading and column headings. Choose an appropriate number of decimal places to print.

1. Generate a table of conversions from degrees to radians. The first line should contain the values for 0°, the second line should contain the values for 10°, and so on. The last line should contain the values for 360°.

2. Generate a table of conversions from centimeters to inches. Start the centimeters column at 0 and increment by 2 cm. The last line should contain the value 50 cm. (Recall that 1 in. = 2.54 cm.)

3. Generate a table of conversions from mi/hr to ft/s. Start the mi/hr column at 0 and increment by 5 mi/hr. The last line should contain the value 65 mi/hr. (Recall that 1 mi. = 5280 ft.)

Currency Conversions. The following currency conversions apply to Problems 4–7:

$1 = 5.045 francs (Fr)

1 yen (Y) = $0.0101239

1.4682 deutsche mark (DM) = $1

4. Generate a table of conversions from francs to dollars. Start the francs column at 5 Fr and increment by 5 Fr. Print 25 lines in the table.

5. Generate a table of conversions from deutsche marks to francs. Start the deutsche marks column at 1 DM and increment by 2 DM. Print 30 lines in the table.

6. Generate a table of conversions from yen to deutsche marks. Start the yen column at 100 Y, and print 25 lines, with the final line containing the value 10000 Y.

7. Generate a table of conversions from dollars to francs, deutsche marks, and yen. Start the column with $1, and increment by $1. Print 50 lines in the table.

Temperature Conversions. The following problems generate temperature conversion tables. Use the following equations that give relationships between temperatures in degrees Fahrenheit (T_F), degrees Celsius (T_C), degrees Kelvin (T_K), and degrees Rankin (T_R):

$$T_F = T_R - 459.67° \text{ R}$$

$$T_F = \frac{9}{5}T_C + 32° \text{ F}$$

$$T_R = \frac{9}{5}T_K$$

8.   Generate a table with the conversions from Fahrenheit to Kelvin for values from 0° F to 200° F. Allow the user to enter the increments in degrees F between lines.

9.   Generate a table with the conversions from Celsius to Rankin. Allow the user to enter the starting temperature and increment between lines. Print 25 lines in the table.

10.   Generate a table with conversions from Celsius to Fahrenheit. Allow the user to enter the starting temperature, the increment between lines, and the number of lines for the table.

3

Courtesy of National Center for Atmospheric Research/
University Corporation for Atmospheric Research/
National Science Foundation.

GRAND CHALLENGE:
Speech Recognition

The modern jet cockpit has literally hundreds of switches and gauges. Several research programs have been looking at the feasibility of using a speech recognition system in the cockpit to serve as a pilot's assistant. The system would respond to verbal requests from the pilot for information such as fuel status or altitude. The pilot would use words from a small vocabulary that the computer had been trained to understand. In addition to understanding a selected set of words, the system would also have to be trained using the speech for the pilot who would be using the system. This training information could be stored on a diskette, and inserted into the computer at the beginning of a flight so that the system could recognize the current pilot. The computer system would also use speech synthesis to respond to the pilot's request for information.

MATLAB *Functions*

OBJECTIVES

The operations of adding, subtracting, multiplying, and dividing are the most fundamental operations used by engineers and scientists. However, we also need to perform other routine operations, such as computing the square root of a value or generating a random number. Thus, we present a number of functions for performing computations and for generating random numbers. Finally, we present several selection statements and functions that allow you to analyze or modify selected values within a matrix.

3.1   Math Functions and Trigonometric Functions

Arithmetic expressions often require computations other than addition, subtraction, multiplication, division, and exponentiation. For example, many expressions require the use of logarithms, exponentials and trigonometric functions. MATLAB allows us to use function references to perform these types of computations instead of requiring us to compute them using the basic arithmetic operations. For example, if we want to compute the sine of an angle and store the result in **b**, we can use the following command:

```
b = sin(angle);
```

The **sin** function assumes that the argument is in radians. If the argument contains a value in degrees, we can convert the degrees to radians within the function reference:

```
b = sin(angle*pi/180);
```

We could also have done the conversion in a separate statement:

```
angle_radians = angle*pi/180;
b = sin(angle_radians);
```

These statements are valid if **angle** is a scalar or if **angle** is a matrix. If **angle** is a matrix, then the function will be applied element-by-element to the values in the matrix.

Function　　Now that you have seen an example using a function, we review the rules regarding them. A **function** is a reference that represents a matrix. The arguments or parameters of the function are contained in parentheses following the name of the function. A function may contain no arguments, one argument, or many arguments, depending on its definition. For example, **pi** is a function that has no argument. When we use the function reference **pi**, the value for π automatically replaces the function reference. If a function contains more than one argument, it is very important to give the arguments in the correct order. Some functions also require that the arguments be in specific units. For example, the trigonometric functions assume that the arguments are in radians. In MATLAB, some functions use the number of arguments to determine the output of the function. Also, function names must be in lowercase.

A function reference cannot be used on the left side of an equal sign because it represents a value and not a variable. Functions can appear on the right side of an equal sign and in expressions. A function reference can also be part of the argument of another function reference. For example, the following statement computes the logarithm of the absolute value of x:

```
log_x = log(abs(x));
```

When one function is used to compute the argument of another function, be sure to enclose the argument of each function in its own set of parentheses. This nesting of functions is also called composition of functions.

We now discuss several categories of functions that are commonly used in engineering computations. Other functions will be presented throughout the remaining chapters as we discuss relevant subjects. Tables of common functions are included on the final two pages of this book.

ELEMENTARY MATH FUNCTIONS

The elementary math functions include functions to perform a number of common computations, such as computing the absolute value and the square root. In addition, we also include a group of functions used to perform rounding. We now list these functions with a brief description.

abs(x) Computes the absolute value of **x**.

sqrt(x) Computes the square root of **x**.

round(x) Rounds **x** to the nearest integer.

Truncates **fix(x)** Rounds (or **truncates**) **x** to the nearest integer toward zero.

floor(x) Rounds **x** to the nearest integer toward $-\infty$.

ceil(x) Rounds **x** to the nearest integer toward ∞.

sign(x) Returns a value of -1 if **x** is less than zero, a value of zero if **x** equals zero, and a value of 1 otherwise.

rem(x,y) Computes the remainder of $\frac{x}{y}$ For example, **rem(25,4)** is 1, and **rem(100,21)** is 16.

exp(x) Computes the value of e^x, where e is the base for natural logarithms, or approximately 2.718282.

log(x) Computes ln **x**, the natural logarithm of **x** to the base e.

log10(x) Computes $\log_{10}x$, the common logarithm of **x** to the base 10.

Practice!

Evaluate the following expressions, and then check your answer by entering the expressions in MATLAB.

1. **round(-2.6)**
2. **fix(-2.6)**
3. **floor(-2.6)**
4. **ceil(-2.6)**
5. **sign(-2.6)**
6. **rem(15,2)**

7.   `floor(ceil(10.8))`
8.   `log10(100) + log10(0.001)`
9.   `abs(-5:5)`
10.   `round([0:0.3:2,1:0.75:4])`

TRIGONOMETRIC FUNCTIONS

The trigonometric functions assume that angles are represented in radians. To convert radians to degrees or degrees to radians, use the following conversions, which use the fact that $180° = \pi$ radians:

```
angle_degrees = angle_radians*(180/pi);
angle_radians = angle_degrees*(pi/180);
```

We now list the trigonometric functions with brief descriptions:

`sin(x)`	Computes the sine of **x**, where **x** is in radians.
`cos(x)`	Computes the cosine of **x**, where **x** is in radians.
`tan(x)`	Computes the tangent of **x**, where **x** is in radians.
`asin(x)`	Computes the arcsine or inverse sine of **x**, where **x** must be between –1 and 1. The function returns an angle in radians between $\frac{-\pi}{2}$ and $\frac{\pi}{2}$
`acos(x)`	Computes the arccosine or inverse cosine of **x**, where **x** must be between –1 and 1. Returns an angle in radians between 0 and π.
`atan(x)`	Computes the arctangent or inverse tangent of **x**. Returns an angle in radians between $\frac{-\pi}{2}$ and $\frac{\pi}{2}$
`atan2(y,x)`	Computes the arctangent or inverse tangent of the value $\frac{x}{y}$ Returns an angle in radians, which will be between $-\pi$ and π, depending on the signs of **x** and **y**.

The other trigonometric functions can be computed using the following equations:

$$\sec x = \frac{1}{\cos x} \qquad \csc x = \frac{1}{\sin x} \qquad \cot x = \frac{1}{\tan x}$$

Practice!

Give MATLAB commands for computing the following values:

1.   Uniformly accelerated motion:

$$\text{motion} = \sqrt{vi^2 + 2 \cdot a \cdot x}$$

2.   Electrical oscillation frequency:

$$\text{frequency} = \frac{1}{\sqrt{\frac{2\pi c}{L}}}$$

3.   Range for a projectile:

$$\text{range} = 2vi^2 \cdot \frac{\sin(b) \cdot \cos(b)}{g}$$

4.   Length contraction:

$$\text{length} = k\sqrt{1 - \left(\frac{y}{c}\right)^2}$$

5.   Volume of a fillet ring:

$$\text{volume} = 2\pi x^2 \left(\left(1 - \frac{\pi}{4}\right) \cdot y - \left(0.8333 - \frac{\pi}{4}\right) \cdot x \right)$$

6.   Distance of the center of gravity from a reference plane in a hollow cylinder sector:

$$\text{center} = \frac{38.1972 \cdot (r^3 - s^3) \sin a}{(r^2 - s^2) \cdot a}$$

3.2   Data Analysis Functions

Analyzing data is an important part of evaluating test results. MATLAB contains a number of functions to make it easier to evaluate and analyze data. We first present a number of simple analysis functions, and then we present functions that compute more complicated measures or metrics related to a data set.

SIMPLE ANALYSIS

The following groups of functions are frequently used in evaluating a set of test data.

Maximum and Minimum. This set of functions can be used to determine maximums and minimums and their locations.

`max(x)`   Returns the largest value in a vector **x**. Returns a row vector containing the maximum element from each column of a matrix **x**.

max(x,y)   Returns a matrix the same size as **x** and **y**. Each element in the matrix contains the maximum value from the corresponding positions in **x** and **y**.

min(x)   Returns the smallest value in a vector **x**. Returns a row vector containing the minimum element from each column of a matrix **x**.

min(x,y)   Returns a matrix the same size as **x** and **y**. Each element in the matrix contains the minimum value from the corresponding positions in **x** and **y**.

Mean

Mean and Median. The **mean** of a group of values is the average. The Greek symbol μ (mu) is used to represent the mean value, as shown in the following equation, which uses summation notation to define the mean:

$$\mu = \frac{\sum_{k=1}^{N} x_k}{n}$$

where $\sum_{k=1}^{N} x_k = x_1 + x_2 + \ldots + x_N$.

Median

The **median** is the value in the middle of the group, assuming that the values are sorted. If there is an odd number of values, the median is the value in the middle position. If there is an even number of values, then the median is the average of the two middle values.

The functions for computing the mean and median are the following:

mean(x)   Computes the mean value (or average value) of the elements of a vector **x**. Computes a row vector that contains the mean value of each column of a matrix **x**.

median(x)   Computes the median value of the elements in a vector **x**. Computes a row vector that contains the median value of each column of a matrix **x**.

Sums and Products. MATLAB contains functions for computing the sums and products of columns in a matrix and functions for computing the cumulative sums and products of the elements in a matrix.

sum(x)   Computes the sum of the elements in a vector **x**. Computes a row vector that contains the sum of each column of a matrix **x**.

prod(x)   Computes the product of the elements in a vector **x**. Computes a row vector that contains the product of each column of a matrix **x**.

cumsum(x)   Computes a vector of the same size containing cumulative sums of values from a vector **x**. Computes a matrix the size as **x** containing cumulative sums of values from the columns of **x**.

cumprod(x)   Computes a vector of the same size containing cumulative products of values from a vector **x**. Computes a matrix the size as **x** containing cumulative products of values from the columns of **x**.

Sorting Values. MATLAB contains a function for sorting values into ascending order.

sort(x)   Sorts the values of a vector **x** into ascending order. Sorts each column of a matrix **x** into ascending order.

Practice!

Determine the matrices represented by the following function references. Then use MATLAB to check your answers. Assume that **w**, **x**, and **y** are the following matrices:

$$w = [0 \ 3 \ {-2} \ 7] \qquad x = [3 \ {-1} \ 5 \ 7]$$

$$y = \begin{bmatrix} 1 & 3 & 7 \\ 2 & 8 & 4 \\ 6 & -1 & -2 \end{bmatrix}$$

1. **max(w)**
2. **min(y)**
3. **min(w,x)**
4. **mean(y)**
5. **median(w)**
6. **cumprod(y)**
7. **sort(2*w+x)**
8. **sort(y)**

VARIANCE AND STANDARD DEVIATION

Two of the most important statistical measurements for a set of data are the variance and standard deviation. Before we give the mathematical definitions, it is useful to develop an intuitive understanding of these values. Consider the values of vectors **data_1** and **data_2** that are plotted in Figure 3.1. If we attempted to draw a line through the middle of the values in the plots, this line would be at approximately 3.0 in both plots. Thus, we would assume that both vectors have approximately the same mean value of 3.0. However, the data in the two vectors clearly have some distinguishing characteristics. The data values in **data_2**

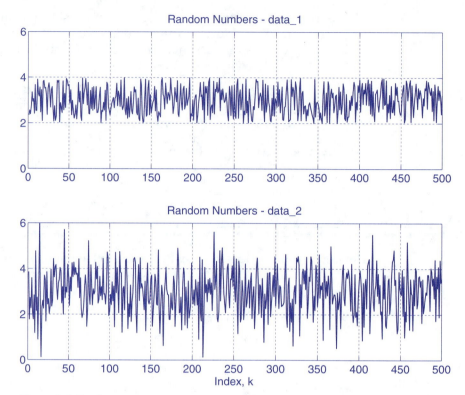

Figure 3.1 *Random sequences.*

vary more from the mean or deviate more from the mean. Thus, measures of variance and deviation for the values in **data_2** will be greater than the variance and deviation for the values in **data_1**. Hence, an intuitive understanding for variance (or deviation) relates to the variance of the values from the mean. The larger the variance, the further the values fluctuate from the mean value.

Variance   Mathematically, the **variance** σ^2 for a set of data values (which we will assume are stored in a vector x) can be computed using the following equation:

$$\sigma^2 = \frac{\displaystyle\sum_{k=1}^{N}(x_k - \mu)^2}{N - 1}$$

This equation is a bit intimidating at first, but if you look at it closely, it becomes much simpler. The term $x_k - \mu$ is the difference or deviation of x_k from the mean. This value is squared so that we will always have a positive value. We then add the squared deviations for all the data points. This sum is then divided by $N - 1$, which approximates an average. (The equation for the variance sometimes uses a denominator of N, but the form here has statistical properties that make it generally more desirable.) Thus, the variance is the average squared deviation of the data from the mean.

Standard deviation

The **standard deviation** is defined to be the square root of the variance, or

$$\sigma = \sqrt{\sigma^2}$$

where σ is the Greek symbol sigma. MATLAB includes a function to compute the standard deviation. To compute the variance, simply square the standard deviation.

std(x)   Computes the standard deviation of the values in a vector **x**. Computes a row vector containing the standard deviation of each column of a matrix **x**.

HISTOGRAMS

Histogram

The **histogram** is a special type of graph that is particularly relevant to the statistical measurements discussed in this section. A histogram is a plot showing the distribution of a set of values. In MATLAB, the histogram computes the number of values falling in ten bins that are equally spaced between the minimum and maximum values from the set of values. For example, if we plot the histograms of the data values in vectors **data_1** and **data_2** (see Figure 3.1), we obtain the histograms in Figure 3.2. Note that the information from a histogram is different from the information obtained from the mean and variance. The histogram shows us not only the range of values, but also how they are distributed. For example, the values in **data_1** tend to be equally distributed across the range of values. (In Section 3.3 we will see that these types of values are called uniformly distributed values.) The values in **data_2** are not equally distributed across the range of values. In fact, most of the values are centered around the mean. (In Section 3.3, we will see that this type of distribution is a Gaussian or normal distribution.)

The MATLAB command to generate and plot a histogram is

```
hist(x)
```

where x is a vector containing the data to be used in the histogram. The **hist** command also allows us to select the number of bins. Therefore, if we want to increase the resolution of the histogram so that 25 bins are used, instead of 10, we use the following equation:

```
hist(x,25)
```

The corresponding plots with 25 bins, using the **data_1** and **data_2** vectors, are shown in Figure 3.3.

3.3   Random Numbers

Simulation

There are many engineering problems that require the use of random numbers in the development of a solution. In some cases, the random numbers are used to develop a **simulation** of a complex problem. The simulation can be tested over

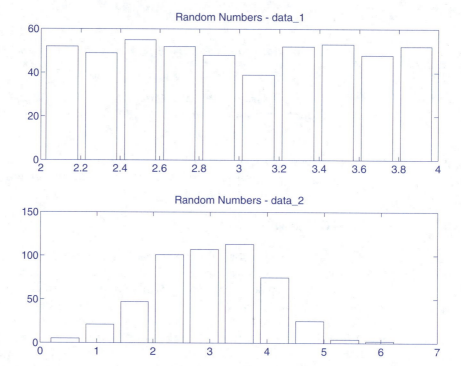

Figure 3.2 *Histograms with 10 bins.*

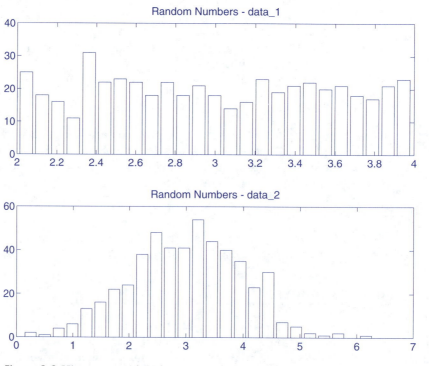

Figure 3.3 *Histograms with 25 bins.*

and over to analyze the results, and each test represents a repetition of the experiment. We also use random numbers to approximate noise sequences. For example, the static that we hear on a radio is a noise sequence. If we are testing a program that uses an input data file that represents a radio signal, we may want to generate noise and add it to a speech signal or a music signal in order to provide a more realistic signal.

UNIFORM RANDOM NUMBERS

Uniform

Random numbers are not defined by an equation; instead they can be characterized by the distribution of values. For example, random numbers that are equally likely to be any value between an upper and lower limit are called **uniform** random numbers. The top histogram in Figure 3.3 on page 66 shows the distribution of a set of uniform values between 2 and 4.

Seed

The **rand** function in MATLAB generates random numbers uniformly distributed over the interval [0,1]. A **seed** value is used to initiate a random sequence of values. This seed value is initially set to zero, but it can be changed with the **rand** function.

`rand(n)`	Returns an $n \times n$ matrix. Each value in the matrix is a random number between 0 and 1.
`rand(m,n)`	Returns an $m \times n$ matrix. Each value in the matrix is a random number between 0 and 1.
`rand('seed',n)`	Sets the value of the seed to the value n. The value of n is initially set to 0.
`rand('seed')`	Returns the current value of the random number generator.

The **rand** function generates the same sequence of random values in each work session if the same seed value is used. The following commands generate and print two sets of ten random numbers uniformly distributed between 0 and 1. The difference between the two sets is caused by the different seeds:

```
rand('seed',0)
set1 = rand(10,1);
rand('seed',123)
set2 = rand(10,1);
[set1 set2]
```

The values printed by these commands are

```
0.2190 0.0878
0.0470 0.6395
0.6789 0.0986
0.6793 0.6906
0.9347 0.3415
0.3835 0.2359
0.5194 0.2641
```

```
0.8310 0.6044
0.0346 0.4181
0.0535 0.1363
```

Random sequences with values that range between values other than 0 and 1 are often needed. To illustrate, suppose that we want to generate values between –5 and 5. We first generate a random number r (which is between 0 and 1) and then multiply it by 10, which is the difference between the upper and lower bounds (5–(–5)). We then add the lower bound (–5), giving a resulting value that is equally likely to be any value between –5 and 5. Thus, if we want to convert a value r, which is uniformly distributed between 0 and 1, to a value uniformly distributed between a lower bound a and an upper bound b, we use the following equation:

$$x = (b - a) \cdot r + a$$

The sequence **data_1**, plotted in Figure 3.1 on page 64, was generated with this equation:

```
data_1 = rand(1,500)*2 + 2;
```

Thus, the sequence contains 500 values uniformly distributed between 2 and 4. The random number seed was 246.

Practice!

Give the MATLAB statements to generate ten random numbers with the specified range. Check your answers by executing the statements and printing the values generated in the vectors.

1. Uniform random numbers between 0 and 10.0.
2. Uniform random numbers between -1 and $+1$.
3. Uniform random numbers between -20 and –10.
4. Uniform random numbers between 4.5 and 5.0.
5. Uniform random numbers between $-\pi$ and π.

GAUSSIAN RANDOM NUMBERS

When we generate a random sequence with a uniform distribution, all values are equally likely to occur. We sometimes need to generate random numbers using distributions in which some values are more likely to be generated than others. For example, suppose that a random sequence represents outdoor temperature

measurements taken over a period of time. We would find that temperature measurements have some variation, but typically are not equally likely. For example,
we might find that the values vary over only a few degrees, although larger
changes could occasionally occur because of storms, cloud shadows, and day-to-
night changes.

Normal random variable

Random sequences that have some values that are more likely to occur than
others can often be modeled with a Gaussian random variable (also called a **normal random variable**). An example of a distribution of a set of values with a
Gaussian distribution is shown in the second plot in Figure 3.3 on page 67. The
mean value of this random variable corresponds to the x coordinate of the peak
of this distribution, which is approximately 3. From this histogram, you can see
that most values are close to the mean. Although a uniform random variable has
specific upper and lower bounds, a Gaussian random variable is not defined in
terms of upper and lower bounds—it is defined in terms of the mean and variance of the values. For Gaussian random numbers, it can be shown that approximately 68% of the values will fall within one standard deviation of the mean,
95% will fall within two standard deviations of the mean, and 99% will fall
within three standard deviations of the mean. These statistics are useful in work-
ing with Gaussian random numbers.

MATLAB will generate Gaussian values with a mean of zero and a variance
of 1.0 if we specify a normal distribution. The functions for generating Gaussian
values are

randn(n)   Returns an $n \times n$ matrix. Each value in the matrix is a
Gaussian (or normal) random number with a mean of zero
and a standard deviation of 1.

randn(m,n)   Returns an $m \times n$ matrix. Each value in the matrix is a
Gaussian (or normal) random number with a mean of zero
and a standard deviation of 1.

To modify Gaussian values with a mean of zero and a variance of 1 to another Gaussian distribution, multiply the values by the standard deviation of the
desired distribution, and add the mean of the desired distribution. Thus, if r is a
random number with a mean of zero and a variance of 1.0, the following equation will generate a new random number with a standard deviation of a and a
mean of b:

$$x = a \cdot r + b$$

The sequence **data_2**, plotted in Figure 3.1 on page 64, was generated with
this equation:

```
data_2 = randn(1,500) + 3;
```

Thus, the sequence contains 500 Gaussian random variables with a standard deviation of 1 and a mean of 3. The random number seed used was 95.

3.4   Problem Solving Applied: Flight Simulator

Computer simulations are used to generate situations that model or emulate a real-world situation. Some computer simulations are written to play games such as checkers, poker, or chess. To play the game, you indicate your move, and the computer will select an appropriate response. Other animated games use computer graphics to develop an interaction as you use the keys or a mouse to play the game. In more sophisticated computer simulations, such as those in a flight simulator, the computer not only responds to the input from the user but also generates values such as temperatures, wind speeds, and the locations of other aircraft. The simulators also simulate emergencies that occur during the flight of an aircraft. If all this information generated by the computer were always the same set of information, the value of the simulator would be greatly reduced. It is important that there be "randomness" to the generation of the data. Simulations that use random numbers to generate values that model events are called **Monte Carlo** simulations.

Monte Carlo

Write a program to generate a random sequence to simulate one hour of wind speed data that is updated every 10 seconds. Assume that the wind speed will be modeled as a uniform random number that varies between a lower limit and an upper limit. Plot the data and save it in an ASCII file named **windspd.dat**.

1.   **PROBLEM STATEMENT**

Generate 1 hour of simulated wind speed data using a lower limit and an upper limit.

2.   **INPUT/OUTPUT**

As shown in I/O diagram below, the inputs to the program are the lower limits and upper limits for the wind speed. The output is the plot and the data file containing the simulated wind speeds.

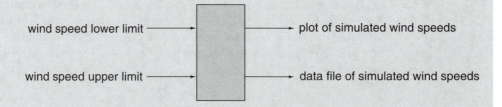

3.   **HAND EXAMPLE**

This simulation uses MATLAB's random number generator to generate numbers between 0 and 1. We then modify these values to be between a specified lower limit and an upper limit. Thus, to generate a value between 10 and 15, we would multiply a random number (between 0 and 1) by 5, and add 10 to it. Hence, the value 0.1 would be converted to 10.5.

4.   MATLAB SOLUTION

```
%   These statements generate one hour of simulated
%   wind speeds based on inputs for the lower
%   and upper limits.
%
low_speed = input('Enter lower limit for wind speed: ');
high_speed = input('Enter upper limit for wind speed: ');
seed = input('Enter seed for random numbers: ');
%
%       Generate simulated wind speed.
%
t = 0:1/360:1;
rand('seed',seed)
speed = (high_speed - low_speed)*rand(1,361) + low_speed;
plot(t,speed),title('Simulated Wind Speed'),
xlabel('t,hours'),ylabel('wind, mi/hr'),grid,pause
data(:,1) = t';
data(:,2) = speed';
save windspd.dat data /ascii
```

5.   TESTING

Figure 3.4 contains plots of the wind speed given the same limits (between 3 and 6 mi/hr) but with different seeds (seeds of 123 and 246).

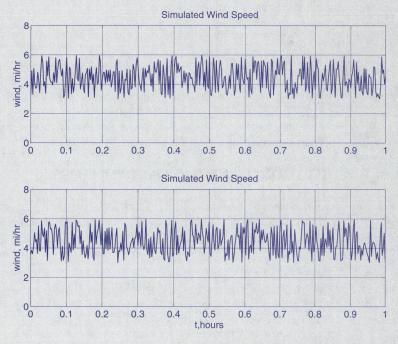

Figure 3.4 *Simulated wind speeds with different random number seeds.*

3.5   Selection Statements and Selection Functions

Conditions

A selection statement allows us to ask a question or test a condition to determine which steps are to be performed next. The **conditions** that are evaluated often contain relational and logical operators, or they contain relational and logical functions. We first discuss the most common form of selection structure—an **if** statement—and then discuss relational and logical operators and functions.

SIMPLE *if* STATEMENT

An example of the **if** statement is shown next:

```
if g<50
    count = count + 1;
    disp(g);
end
```

Assume that **g** is a scalar. If **g<50**, then **count** is incremented by 1, and **g** is displayed on the screen; otherwise, these two statements are skipped. If **g** is not a scalar, then **count** is incremented by 1, and **g** is displayed only if every element in **g** is less than 50.

The general form of a simple **if** statement is the following:

```
if logical expression
    statements
end
```

If the logical expression is true, we execute the statements between the **if** statement and the **end** statement. If the logical expression is false, we jump immediately to the statement following the **end** statement. It is important to indent the statements within an **if** structure for readability.

Because logical expressions are generated from relational operators and logical operators, we now discuss these new operators.

RELATIONAL AND LOGICAL OPERATORS

MATLAB has six relational operators for comparing two matrices of equal size, as shown in Table 3.1. Matrices or matrix expressions are used on both sides of a relational operator to yield another matrix of the same size. Each entry in the resulting matrix contains a 1 if the comparison is true when applied to the values in the corresponding position of the matrices; otherwise, the entry in the resulting matrix contains a 0. An expression that contains a relational operator is a logical expression because the result is a matrix containing zeros and ones, which can be interpreted as false values and true values, respectively; the resulting matrix is also called a **0–1 matrix**.

0-1 matrix

TABLE 3.1 Relational Operators	
Relational Operator	**Interpretation**
<	less than
<=	less than or equal
>	greater than
>=	greater than or equal
==	equal
~=	not equal

Consider the following logical expression **a<b**. If **a** and **b** are scalars, the value of this expression is 1 (for true) if **a** is less than **b**; otherwise, the expression is 0 (for false). Let **a** and **b** be vectors with the following values:

$$a = [2\ 4\ 6] \qquad b = [3\ 5\ 1]$$

Then, the value of **a<b** is the vector [1 1 0], and the value **of a~=b** is **[1 1 1]**.

We can also combine two logical expressions, using the logical operators *not*, *and*, and *or*. These logical operators are represented by the symbols shown in Table 3.2. Logical operators allow us to compare 0–1 matrices such as those computed by relational operators, as shown in the following logical expression:

a<b & b<c

TABLE 3.2 Logical Operators	
Logical Operator	**Symbol**
not	~
and	&
or	|

This operation is valid only if the two resultant matrices (represented by **a<b** and **b<c**) are the same size. Then, an entry in the matrix represented by this logical expression is 1 if the values in the corresponding entries in **a**, **b**, and **c** are such that **a<b<c**; otherwise, the entry is zero.

When two logical expressions are joined by **|**, an entry in the resulting 0–1 matrix is 1 (true) if either or both expressions are true; it is 0 (false) only when both expressions are false. When two logical expressions are joined by **&**, the entire expression is true only if both expressions are true. Table 3.3 lists all possible combinations for the logical operators with two logical expressions.

Logical operators are used with complete logical expressions. For example, **a>b & b>c** is a valid logical expression, but **a>b & c** is not an equivalent expression. Logical expressions can also be preceded by the logical operator not. This operator changes the value of the expression to the opposite value; hence, if **a>b** is true, then **~(a>b)** is false.

TABLE 3.3 Combinations of Logical Operators

A	B	~A	A | B	A & B
false	false	true	false	false
false	true	true	true	false
true	false	false	true	false
true	true	false	true	true

A logical expression may contain several logical operators, as in

~(b==c | b==5.5)

The hierarchy, from highest to lowest is ~, &, and |. Of course, parentheses can be used to change the hierarchy. In the example above, the expressions b==c and b==5.5 are evaluated first. Suppose b contains the value 3 and c contains the value 5. Then neither expression is true, so the expression b==c | b==5.5 is false. We then apply the ~ operator, which changes the value of the expression to true. Suppose that we did not have the parentheses around the logical expression, as in

~ b==c | b==5.5

In this case, the expression ~b==c would be evaluated along with b==5.5. For the values given for b and c, the value of each relational expression is false; thus, the value of the entire logical expression is false. You might wonder how we can evaluate ~b when the value in b is a number. In MATLAB, any values that are nonzero are considered to be true; values of zero are false. As a result, we have to be very careful using relational and logical operators to be sure that the steps being performed are the ones that we want to perform.

Practice!

Determine if the following expressions in problems 1 through 8 are true or false. Then check your answers using MATLAB. Remember that to check your answer, all you need to do is enter the expression. Assume that the following variables have the indicated values:

a = 5.5   b = 1.5   k = -3

1.   a < 10.0
2.   a+b >= 6.5
3.   k ~= 0
4.   b-k > a

```
5.    ~(a == 3*b)
6.    -k <= k+6
7.    a<10 & a>5
8.    abs(k)>3  |  k<b-a
```

NESTED *if* STATEMENTS

Here is an example of nested **if** statements that extends the previous example:

```
if g < 50
    count = count + 1;
    disp(g);
    if b > g
        b = 0;
    end
end
```

Again, first assume that **g** and **b** are scalars. Then, if **g > 50**, we increment **count** by 1 and display **g**. In addition, if **b > g**, then we also set **b** to zero. If **g** is not less than 50, then we skip immediately to the statement following the second **end** statement. If **g** is not a scalar, then the condition **g < 50** is true only if every element of **g** is less than 50. If neither **g** nor **b** is a scalar, then **b** is greater than **g** only if every corresponding pair of elements of **g** and **b** are values such that **b** is greater than **g**. If **g** or **b** is a scalar, then the other matrix is compared to the scalar element-wise.

else AND *elseif* CLAUSES

The **else** clause allows us to execute one set of statements if a logical expression is true and a different set if the logical expression is false. To illustrate this statement, assume that we have a variable **interval**. If the value of **interval** is less than 1, we set the value of **x_increment** to **interval/10**; otherwise, we set the value of **x_increment** to 0.1. The following statement performs these steps:

```
if interval < 1
    x_increment = interval/10;
else
    x_increment = 0.1;
end
```

When we nest several levels of **if-else** statements, it may be difficult to determine which logical expressions must be true (or false) to execute each set of statements. In these cases, the **elseif** clause is often used to clarify the program logic, as illustrated in this statement:

```
if temperature > 100
    disp('Too hot - equipment malfunctioning.')
elseif temperature > 90
    disp('Normal operating range.')
elseif temperature > 50
    disp('Temperature below desired operating range.')
else
    disp('Too Cold - turn off equipment.')
end
```

In this example, temperatures above 90 and below or equal to 100 are in the normal operating range. Temperatures outside this range generate an appropriate message.

Practice!

In problems 1 through 4, give MATLAB statements that perform the steps indicated. Assume that the variables are scalars.

1. If the difference between **volt_1** and **volt_2** is larger than 10.0, print the values of **volt_1** and **volt_2**.

2. If the natural logarithm of **x** is greater than or equal to 3, set **time** equal to zero and increment **count**.

3. If **dist** is less than 50.0 and **time** is greater than 10.0, increment **time** by 2; otherwise, increment **time** by 2.5.

4. If **dist** is greater than or equal to 100.0, increment **time** by 2.0. If **dist** is between 50 and 100, increment **time** by 1. Otherwise, increment **time** by 0.5.

LOGICAL FUNCTIONS

MATLAB contains a set of logical functions that are very useful with **if** statements. We now discuss each of these functions.

any(x)   Returns a scalar that is 1 (true) if any element in the vector **x** is nonzero; otherwise, the scalar is zero (false). Returns a row vector if **x** is a matrix. An element in this row vector contains a 1 (true) if any element of the corresponding column of **x** is nonzero and a zero (false) otherwise.

all(x)   Returns a scalar that is 1 (true) if all elements in the vector **x** are nonzero; otherwise, the scalar is zero (false). Returns a row vector if **x** is a matrix. An element in this row vector contains a 1 (true) if all elements of the corresponding column of **x** are nonzero and a zero (false) otherwise.

find(x)   Returns a vector containing the indices of the nonzero elements of a vector **x**. If **x** is a matrix, the indices are selected from **x(:)**, which is a long column vector formed from the columns of **x**.

isnan(x)   Returns a matrix with ones where the elements of **x** are NaNs and zeros where they are not.

finite(x)   Returns a matrix with ones where the elements of **x** are finite and zeros where they are infinite or NaN.

isempty(x)   Returns 1 if **x** is an empty matrix and 0 otherwise.

Assume that **A** is a matrix with three rows and three columns of values. Consider the following statement:

```
if all(A)
   disp ('A contains no zeros')
end
```

The string **A contains no zeros** is printed only if all nine values in **A** are nonzero.

We now present another example that uses a logical function. Assume that we have a vector **d** containing a group of distance values that represent the distances of a cable car from the nearest tower. We want to generate a vector containing corresponding velocities of the cable car. If the cable car is within 30 feet of the tower, we use this equation to compute the velocity:

$$\text{velocity} = 0.425 + 0.00175 \cdot d^2$$

If the cable car is further than 30 feet from the tower, we use the following equation:

$$\text{velocity} = 0.625 + 0.12d - 0.00025d^2$$

We can use the **find** function to find the distance values greater than 30 feet and to find the distance values less than or equal to 30 feet. Because the **find** function identifies the subscripts for each group of values, we can then compute the corresponding velocities with these statements:

```
lower = find(d < 30);
velocity(lower) = 0.425 + 0.00175*d(lower).^2;
upper = find(d >= 30);
velocity(upper) = 0.625 + 0.12*d(upper)...
                   - 0.00025*d(upper).^2;
```

If all the values of **d** are less than 30, the vector **upper** will be an empty vector, and the reference to **d(upper)** and **velocity(upper)** will not cause any values to change.

Practice!

Determine the value of the following expressions. Then check your answers using MATLAB. Remember that to check your answer, all you need to do is enter the expression. Assume that the matrix **b** has the indicated values:

$$b = \begin{bmatrix} 1 & 0 & 4 \\ 0 & 0 & 3 \\ 8 & 7 & 0 \end{bmatrix}$$

1. `any(b)`
2. `find(b)`
3. `all(any(b))`
4. `any(all(b))`
5. `finite(b(:,3))`
6. `any(b(1:2,1:3))`

LOOPS

A loop is structure that allows you to repeat a set of statements. In general, you should avoid loops in MATLAB because they are seldom needed and they can significantly increase the execution time of a program. However, there are occasions when loops are needed, so we give a brief introduction to **for** loops and **while** loops.

In the example at the end of the previous discussion, we used the **find** function to find distance values greater the 30 feet, and distance values less than or equal to 30 feet. We then computed the corresponding velocites using the appropriate equations. Another way to perform these steps uses a **for** loop. In the following statements, the value of **k** is set to 1, and the statements inside the loop are executed. The value of **k** is incremented to 2, and the statements inside the loop are executed again. This continues until the value of **k** is greater than the length of the **d** vector.

```
for k = 1:length(d)
   if d(k) < 30
      velocity(k) = 0.425 - 0.00175*d(k).^2;
   else
      velocity(k) = 0.625 + 0.12*d(k) ...
                    - 0.00025*d(k).^2;
   end
end
```

While these statements perform the same operations as the steps using the **find** function, the solution without a loop will execute much faster.

A **for** loop has the following general structure:

```
for index = expression
    statements
end
```

The expression is a matrix (which could be a scalar or a vector), and the statements are repeated as many times as there are columns in the expression matrix. Each time through the loop, the index has the value of one of the elements in the expression matrix. The rules for writing and using a **for** loop are the following:

1. The index of a **for** loop must be a variable.
2. If the expression matrix is the empty matrix, a loop will not be executed. Control will pass to the statement following the **end** statement.
3. If the expression matrix is a scalar, a loop will be executed one time, with the index containing the value of the scalar.
4. If the expression matrix is a row vector, each time through a loop, the index will contain the next value in the vector.
5. If the expression matrix is a matrix, each time through a loop, the index will contain the next column in the matrix.
6. Upon completion of a **for** loop, the index contains the last value used.
7. The colon operator can be used to define the expression matrix using the following format:

```
for k = initial:increment:limit
```

Practice!

Determine the number of times that a **for** loop defined by the following statements will be executed. Then, to check your answer, use the **length** function, which returns the number of values in a vector. Thus, the number of times that the **for** loop in problem 1 is executed is **length(3:20)**.

1.	`for k = 3:20`	4.	`for time = 10:-1:0`
2.	`for count = -2:14`	5.	`for time = 10:5`
3.	`for k = -2:-1:-10`	6.	`for index = 2:3:12`

The **while** loop is a structure for repeating a set of statements as long as a specified condition is true. The general format for this control structure is

```
while expression
    statements
end
```

If the expression is true, the statements are executed. After these statements are executed, the condition is retested. If the condition is still true, the group of statements is executed again. When the condition is false, control skips to the statement following the **end** statement. The variables modified in the statements should include the variables in the expression, or the value of the expression will never change. If the expression is always true (or is a value that is nonzero), the loop becomes an infinite loop.

3.6   User-Written Functions

As you use MATLAB to perform more and more computations, you will find calculations that you wish were included as functions in MATLAB. In these cases, you can write the function in an M-file, and then your program can refer to the function in the same way that it refers to a MATLAB function. The function file has very specific rules that must be followed when writing it. Before we list the rules, we consider a simple example.

The sinc function is a function commonly used in many engineering applications. Unfortunately, there are two widely-accepted definitions for this function, as shown below:

$$f_1(x) = \frac{\sin \pi x}{\pi x} \quad f_2(x) = \frac{\sin x}{x}$$

Both of these functions have an indeterminate form of 0/0 when x is equal to zero. In this case l'Hôpital's theorem from calculus can be used to prove that both functions are equal to 1 when x is equal to zero. For values of x not equal to zero, these two functions have similar form, but the first function crosses the x-axis when x is an integer and the second function crosses the x-axis when x is a multiple of π. A MATLAB **sinc** function that uses the first definition is included in the Signal Processing Toolbox and in the Student Edition Version 4. Assume that you would like to define another function called **sinc_x** that would use the second definition, which is shown in Figure 3.5. The following function can be used to compute this alternative form of the sinc function, where x can be a scalar, vector, or matrix.

```
function s = sinc_x(x)
%
% SINC_X This function computes the value of sin(x)/x
%
s = x;
set1 = find(abs(x)<0.001);
set2 = find(abs(x)>=0.001);
s(set1) = ones(size(set1));
s(set2) = sin(x(set2))./x(set2);
```

This function should saved in a file named **sinc_x.m**. Then, MATLAB programs and scripts can refer to this function in same way that they refer to functions such as **sqrt** and **abs**. The figure shown in Figure 3.5 was plotted using these statements:

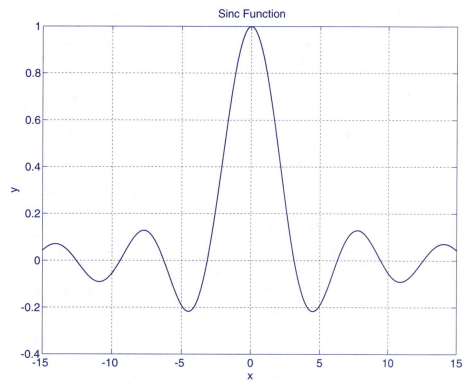

Figure 3.5 *Sinc function in interval [–15, 15]*

```
% Statements to generate Figure 3.6.
%
x = -15:0.1:15;
y = sinc_x(x);
plot(x,y),title('Sinc Function'),
xlabel('x'),ylabel('y'),grid,pause
```

We now summarize the rules for writing an M-file function. Refer to the **sinc_x** function as you read each rule.

1.   The function must begin with a line containing the word **function**, which is followed by the output argument, an equal sign, and the name of the function. The input arguments to the function follow the function name and are enclosed in parentheses. This line distinguishes the function file from a script file.

2.   The first few lines should be comments because they will be displayed if help is requested for the function name, as in **help sinc_x**.

3.   The only information returned from the function is contained in the output arguments, which are, of course, matrices. Always check to be sure that the function includes a statement that assigns a value to the output argument.

4. The same matrix names can be used in both a function and the program that references it. No confusion occurs as to which matrix is referenced because the function and the program are completely separate. However, any values computed in the function, other than the output arguments, are not accessible from the program.

5. A function that is going to return more than one value should show all values to be returned as a vector in the function statement, as in this example, which will return three values:

```
function [dist, vel, accel] = motion(x)
```

All three values need to be computed within the function.

6. A function that has multiple input arguments must list the arguments in the function statement, as shown in this example, which has two input arguments:

```
function error = mse(w,d)
```

7. The special variables **nargin** and **nargout** can be used to determine the number of input arguments and the number of output arguments for a function.

The **what** command lists all the M-files and MAT files that are available in the current workspace. The **type** command followed by a file name will display the contents of a file on the screen. If an extension is not included with the file name, the **type** command automatically assumes that the extension is **.m**.

CHAPTER SUMMARY

In this chapter we explored the various MATLAB functions for creating matrices and for calculating new matrices from existing matrices. These functions included mathematical functions, trigonometric functions, data analysis functions, random number generation functions, and logical functions. In addition, we presented selection statements and functions so that we can analyze or modify selected portions of matrices. A brief discussion of loops was included because they are occasionally needed in MATLAB solutions. Finally we, illustrated the steps in developing a user-written function.

MATLAB SUMMARY

This MATLAB summary lists all the special character, commands, and functions that were defined in this chapter. A brief description is also included for each one.

SPECIAL CHARACTERS

<	less than
<=	less than or equal
>	greater than
>=	greater than or equal
==	equal
~=	not equal
&	and
|	or
~	not

COMMANDS AND FUNCTIONS

abs	computes absolute value or magnitude
acos	computes arccosine
all	determines if all values are true
any	determines if any values are true
asin	computes arcsine
atan	computes 2-quadrant arctangent
atan2	computes 4-quadrant arctangent
ceil	rounds towards ∞
cos	computes cosine of angle
cumprod	determines cumulative products
cumsum	determines cumulative sums
else	optional clause in if structure
elseif	optional clause in if structure
end	defines end of a control structure
exp	computes value with base e
find	locates nonzero values
finite	determines if values are finite
fix	rounds toward zero
floor	rounds toward $-\infty$
for	generates loop structure
function	generates user-defined function
hist	plots histogram
if	tests logical expression
isempty	determines if matrix is empty
isnan	determines if values are NaNs

length	determines number of values in a vector
log	computes natural logarithm
log10	computes common logarithm
max	determines maximum value
mean	determines mean value
median	determines median value
min	determines minimum value
prod	determines product of values
rand	generates a uniform random number
randn	generates a Gaussian random number
rem	computes remainder from division
round	rounds to nearest integer
sign	generates –1,0,1 based on sign
sin	computes sine of angle
sort	sorts values
sqrt	computes square root
std	computes standard deviation
sum	determines sum of values
tan	computes tangent of angle
what	lists variables
while	generates a loop structure

PROBLEMS

Rocket Trajectory. A small rocket is being designed to make wind shear measurements in the vicinity of thunderstorms. Before testing begins, the designers are developing a simulation of the rocket's trajectory. They have derived the following equation that they believe will predict the performance of the test rocket, where t is the elapsed time in seconds:

$$\text{height} = 60 + 2.13t^2 - 0.0013t^4 + 0.000034t^{4.751}$$

The equation gives the height above ground level at time t. The first term (60) is the height in feet above ground level of the nose of the rocket.

1. Give the commands to compute and print the time and height of the rocket from $t = 0$ to the time that it hits the ground, in increments of 2 seconds. If the rocket has not hit the ground within 100 seconds, print values only up through 100 seconds.

2. Modify the steps in problem 1 so that instead of a table, the program prints the time at which the rocket begins falling back to the ground and the time at which the rocket impacts.

Suture Packaging. Sutures are strands or fibers used to sew living tissue together after an injury or an operation. Packages of sutures must be sealed carefully before they are shipped to hospitals so that contaminants cannot enter the packages. The object that seals the package is referred to as a sealing die. Generally, sealing dies are heated with an electric heater. For the sealing process to be a success, the sealing die is maintained at an established temperature and must contact the package with a predetermined pressure for an established time period. The time period in which the sealing die contacts the package is called the dwell time. Assume that the acceptable range of parameters for an acceptable seal are the following:

Temperature: 150–170°

Pressure: 60–70psi

Dwell Time: 2–2.5s

3.   A data file named **suture.dat** contains information on batches of sutures that have been rejected during a one-week period. Each line in the data file contains the batch number, the temperature, the pressure, and the dwell time for a rejected batch. A quality control engineer would like to analyze this information to determine the percent of the batches rejected due to temperature, the percent rejected due to pressure, and the percent rejected due to dwell time. If a specific batch is rejected for more than one reason, it should be counted in all applicable totals. Give the MATLAB statements to compute and print these three percentages. Use the following data:

Batch Number	Temperature	Pressure	Dwell Time
24551	145.5	62.3	2.23
24582	153.7	63.2	2.52
26553	160.3	58.9	2.51
26623	159.5	58.9	2.01
26642	160.3	61.2	1.98

4.   Modify the solution developed in problem 3 so that it also prints the number of batches in each rejection category and the total number of batches rejected. (Remember that a rejected batch should appear only once in the total, but could appear in more that one rejection category.)

5.   Write a program to read the data file **suture.dat** and make sure that the information relates only to batches that should have been rejected. If any batch should not be in the data file, print an appropriate message with the batch information.

Timber Regrowth. A problem in timber management is to determine how much of an area to leave uncut so that the harvested area is reforested in a certain period of time. It is assumed that reforestation takes place at a known rate per year, depending on climate and soil conditions. A reforestation equation expresses this growth as a function of the amount of timber standing and the reforestation rate. For example, if 100 acres are left standing after harvesting and the reforestation rate is 0.05, then $100 + 0.05 \times 100$, or 105 acres, are forested at the end of the first year. At the end of the second year, the number of acres forested is $105 + 0.05 \times 105$, or 110.25 acres.

6. Assume that there are 14,000 acres total with 2500 acres uncut, and that the reforestation rate is 0.02. Print a table showing the number of acres reforested at the end of each year, for a total of 20 years.

7. Modify the program developed in problem 6 so that the user can enter the number of years to be used for the table.

8. Modify the program developed in problem 6 so that the user can enter a number of acres, and the program will determine how many years are required for the number of acres to be forested.

Sensor Data. Suppose that a data file named **sensor.dat** contains information collected from a set of sensors. Each row contains a set of sensor readings, with the first row containing values collected at 0.0 seconds, the second row containing values collected at 1.0 seconds, and so on.

9. Write a program to read the data file and print the number of sensors and the number of seconds of data contained in the file.

10. Write a program to preprocess the sensor data so that all values that are greater than 10.0 are set to 10.0, and all values less than −10.0 are set to −10.0.

11. Write a program to print the subscripts of sensor data values with absolute values greater than 20.0.

12. Write a program to print the percentage of sensor data values that are zero.

Power Plant Output. The power output in megawatts from a power plant over a period of eight weeks has been stored in a data file named **plant.dat**. Each line in the data file represents data for one week and contains the output for day 1, day 2, . . . , day 7.

13. Write a program that uses the power plant output data and prints a report that lists the number of days with greater-than-average power output. The report should give the week number and the day number for each of these days, in addition to printing the average power output for the plant during the eight-week period.

14. Write a program that uses the power plant output data and prints the day and week during which the maximum and minimum power output oc-

curred. If the maximum or minimum occurred on more than one day, print all the days involved.

15. Write a program that uses the power plant output data and prints the average power output for each week. Also print the average power output for day 1, day 2, and so on.

4

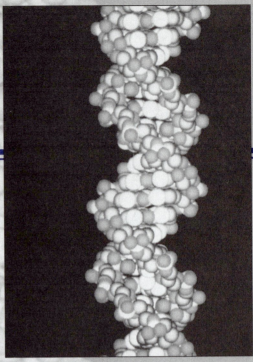

Courtesy of Rainbow.

GRAND CHALLENGE:
Mapping the Human Genome

The deciphering of the human genetic code involves locating, identifying, and determining the function of each of the 50,000 to 100,000 genes that are contained in human DNA. Each gene is a double-helix strand composed of base pairs of adenine bonded with thymine, or cytosine bonded with guanine, that are arranged in a step-like manner with phosphate groups along the side. DNA directs the production of proteins, so the proteins produced by a cell provide a key to the sequence of base pairs in the DNA. Instrumentation developed for genetic engineering is extremely useful in this detective work. A protein sequencer developed in 1969 can identify the sequence of amino acids in a protein molecule. Once the amino acid order is known, biologists can begin to identify the gene that made the protein. A DNA synthesizer, developed in 1982, can build small genes or gene fragments out of DNA. This research, and its associated instrumentation, are key components in beginning to address the mapping of the human genome.

Matrix Computations

4.1   Matrix Operations and Functions

4.2   Solutions to Systems of Linear Equations

Chapter Summary, MATLAB Summary, Problems

OBJECTIVES

A matrix is a convenient way to represent engineering data. In previous chapters, we discussed mathematical computations and functions that could be applied element-by-element to values in matrices. In this chapter we present a set of matrix operations and functions that apply to the matrix as a unit, as opposed to individual elements in the matrix. We first consider a set of mathematical computations that compute new values from a matrix (or matrices). We then present methods for solving a system of simultaneous equations.

4.1   Matrix Operations and Functions

Many engineering computations use a matrix as a convenient way to represent a set of data. In this chapter, we are generally concerned with matrices that have more than one row and more than one column. Recall that scalar multiplication and matrix addition and subtraction are performed element-by-element and were covered in Chapter 2 in the discussion of array operations. Matrix multiplication is covered in this section. Matrix division is presented in the next section and is used to compute the solution to a set of simultaneous linear equations.

TRANSPOSE

Transpose

The **transpose** of a matrix is a new matrix in which the rows of the original matrix are the columns of the new matrix. We use a superscript T after a matrix name to refer to the transpose. For example, consider the following matrix and its transpose:

$$A = \begin{bmatrix} 2 & 5 & 1 \\ 7 & 3 & 8 \\ 4 & 5 & 21 \\ 16 & 13 & 0 \end{bmatrix} \qquad A^T = \begin{bmatrix} 2 & 7 & 4 & 16 \\ 5 & 3 & 5 & 13 \\ 1 & 8 & 21 & 0 \end{bmatrix}$$

If we consider a couple of the elements, we see that the value in position (3,1) of A has now moved to position (1,3) of A^T, and the value in position (4,2) of A has now moved to position (2,4) of A^T. In general, the row and column subscripts are interchanged to form the transpose; hence, the value in position (i,j) is moved to position (j,i).

In MATLAB the transpose of the matrix **A** is denoted by **A'**. Observe that the transpose will have a different size than the original matrix if the original matrix is not a square matrix. We frequently use the transpose operation to convert a row vector to a column vector or a column vector to a row vector.

DOT PRODUCT

Dot product

The **dot product** is a scalar computed from two vectors of the same size. This scalar is the sum of the products of the values in corresponding positions in the vectors, as shown in the summation equation, which assumes that there are N elements in the vectors A and B:

$$\text{dot product} = A \cdot B = \sum_{i=1}^{N} a_i b_i$$

To illustrate, assume that A and B are the following vectors:

$$A = \begin{bmatrix} 4 & -1 & 3 \end{bmatrix} \qquad B = \begin{bmatrix} -2 & 5 & 2 \end{bmatrix}$$

The dot product is then

$$\begin{aligned} A \cdot B &= 4 \cdot (-2) + (-1) \cdot 5 + 3 \cdot 2 \\ &= (-8) + (-5) + 6 \\ &= -7 \end{aligned}$$

In MATLAB, we can compute the dot product with the following statement:

```
dot_product = sum(A.*B);
```

Recall that `A.*B` contains the results of an element-wise multiplication of `A` and `B`. When `A` and `B` are both row vectors or are both column vectors, `A.*B` is also a vector. We then sum the elements in this vector, thus yielding the dot product.

MATRIX MULTIPLICATION

Matrix multiplication is not computed by multiplying corresponding elements of the matrices. In matrix multiplication, the value in position $c(i,j)$ of the product C of two matrices A and B is the dot product of row i of the first matrix and column j of the second matrix, as shown in the summation equation:

$$c_{i,j} = \sum_{k=1}^{N} a_{ik} b_{kj}$$

Because the dot product requires that the vectors have the same number of elements, the first matrix (A) must have the same number of elements (N) in each row as there are in the columns of the second matrix (B). Thus, if A and B both have five rows and five columns, their product has five rows and five columns. Furthermore, for these matrices, we can compute both AB and BA, but in general, they will not be equal.

If A has two rows and three columns, and B has three rows and three columns, the product AB will have two rows and three columns. To illustrate, consider the following matrices:

$$A = \begin{bmatrix} 2 & 5 & 1 \\ 0 & 3 & -1 \end{bmatrix} \qquad B = \begin{bmatrix} 1 & 0 & 2 \\ -1 & 4 & -2 \\ 5 & 2 & 1 \end{bmatrix}$$

The first element in the product $C = AB$ is

$$c_{1,1} = \sum_{k=1}^{3} a_{1k}b_{k1}$$
$$= a_{1,1}b_{1,1} + a_{1,2}b_{2,1} + a_{1,3}b_{3,1}$$
$$= 2 \cdot 1 + 5 \cdot (-1) + 1 \cdot 5$$
$$= 2$$

Similarly, we can compute the rest of the elements in the product of A and B:

$$AB = C = \begin{bmatrix} 2 & 22 & -5 \\ -8 & 10 & -7 \end{bmatrix}$$

In this example, we cannot compute BA because B does not have the same number of elements in each row as A has in each column.

An easy way to decide if a matrix product exists is to write the sizes of the two matrices side by side. Then if the two inside numbers are the same, the product exists, and the size of the product is determined by the two outside numbers. To illustrate, in the previous example, the size of A is 2×3 and the size of B is 3×3. Therefore, if we want to compute AB we write the sizes side-by-side:

$$2 \times 3, 3 \times 3$$

The two inner numbers are both the value 3, so AB exists, and its size is determined by the two outer numbers, 2×3. If we want to compute BA, we again write the sizes side-by-side:

$$3 \times 3, 2 \times 3$$

The two inner numbers are not the same, so BA does not exist.

In MATLAB, matrix multiplication is denoted by an asterisk. Thus, the commands to generate the matrices in our previous example and then compute the matrix product are

```
A = [2,5,1; 0,3,-1];
B = [1,0,2; -1,4,-2; 5,2,1];
C = A*B;
```

If we execute the MATLAB command c = B*A, we get a warning message that c does not exist.

Assume that I is a square identity matrix. (Recall from Chapter 2 that an identity matrix is a matrix with ones on the main diagonal and zeros elsewhere.) If A is a square matrix of the same size, then AI and IA are both equal to A. Use a small matrix A, and verify by hand that these matrix products are both equal to A.

MATRIX POWERS

Recall that if A is a matrix, then A.^2 is the operation that squares each element in the matrix. If we want to square the matrix, that is, to compute A*A, we use the operation A^2. A^4 is equivalent to A*A*A*A. To perform a matrix multiplication between two matrices, the number of rows in the first matrix must be the same value as the number of columns in the second matrix. Therefore, to raise a matrix to a power, the number of rows must equal the number of columns, and, thus, the matrix must be a square matrix.

MATRIX INVERSE

Inverse

By definition, the **inverse** of a square matrix A is the matrix A^{-1} such that the matrix products AA^{-1} and $A^{-1}A$ are both equal to the identity matrix. For example, consider the following two matrices, A and B:

$$A = \begin{bmatrix} 2 & 1 \\ 4 & 3 \end{bmatrix} \qquad B = \begin{bmatrix} 1.5 & -0.5 \\ -2 & 1 \end{bmatrix}$$

If we compute the products AB and BA, we obtain the following matrices. (Do the matrix multiplications by hand to be sure you follow the steps.)

$$AB = \begin{bmatrix} 1 & 0 \\ 0 & 1 \end{bmatrix} \qquad BA = \begin{bmatrix} 1 & 0 \\ 0 & 1 \end{bmatrix}$$

Therefore, A and B are inverses of each other, or $A = B^{-1}$ and $B = A^{-1}$.

Computing the inverse is a tedious process; fortunately, MATLAB contains an **inv** function that performs the computations for us. (We do not present the steps for computing an inverse in this text. Refer to a linear algebra text if you are interested in the techniques for computing an inverse.) Thus, if we execute **inv(A)**, using the A matrix defined above, the result will be the matrix B. Similarly, if we execute **inv(B)**, the result should be the matrix A. Try this yourself.

Singular

There are matrices for which an inverse does not exist; these matrices are called **singular** or ill-conditioned matrices. When you attempt to compute the inverse of an ill-conditioned matrix in MATLAB, an error message is printed.

DETERMINANTS

Determinant

A **determinant** is a scalar computed from the entries in a square matrix. Determinants have various applications in engineering, including computing inverses and solving systems of simultaneous equations. For a 2×2 matrix A, the determinant is

determinant of $A = |A| = a_{1,1}a_{2,2} - a_{2,1}a_{1,2}$

Therefore, the determinant of A, or |A|, is equal to 8 for the following matrix:

$$A = \begin{bmatrix} 1 & 3 \\ -1 & 5 \end{bmatrix}$$

For a 3×3 matrix A, the determinant is the following:

$$|A| = a_{1,1}a_{2,2}a_{3,3} + a_{1,2}a_{2,3}a_{3,1} + a_{1,3}a_{2,1}a_{3,2} - a_{3,1}a_{2,2}a_{1,3} - a_{3,2}a_{2,3}a_{1,1} - a_{3,3}a_{2,1}a_{1,2}$$

If A is the following matrix,

$$A = \begin{bmatrix} 1 & 3 & 0 \\ -1 & 5 & 2 \\ 1 & 2 & 1 \end{bmatrix}$$

then |A| is equal to $5 + 6 + 0 - 0 - 4 - (-3)$, or 10.

A more involved process is necessary for computing determinants of matrices with more than three rows and columns. We do not include the discussion of the process for computing a general determinant here because MATLAB will automatically compute a determinant using the **det** function, with a square matrix as its argument, as in **det(A)**.

Practice!

Use MATLAB to define the following matrices. Then compute the specified matrices if they exist.

$$A = \begin{bmatrix} 2 & 1 \\ 0 & -1 \\ 3 & 0 \end{bmatrix} \qquad B = \begin{bmatrix} 1 & 3 \\ -1 & 5 \end{bmatrix}$$

$$C = \begin{bmatrix} 3 & 2 \\ -1 & -2 \\ 0 & 2 \end{bmatrix} \qquad D = \begin{bmatrix} 1 & 2 \end{bmatrix} \qquad I = \begin{bmatrix} 1 & 0 \\ 0 & 1 \end{bmatrix}$$

1. **DB**
2. **BC^T**
3. **(CB)D^T**
4. **B^{-1}B**
5. **AC^T**
6. **(AC^T)$^{-1}$**
7. **det(B)**
8. **det(A*C^T)**

4.2   Solutions to Systems of Linear Equations

Consider the following system of three equations with three unknowns:

$$
\begin{array}{rrrcr}
3x & +2y & -z & = & 10 \\
-x & +3y & +2z & = & 5 \\
x & -y & -z & = & -1
\end{array}
$$

We can rewrite this system of equations using the following matrices:

$$
A = \begin{bmatrix} 3 & 2 & -1 \\ -1 & 3 & 2 \\ 1 & -1 & -1 \end{bmatrix} \qquad X = \begin{bmatrix} x \\ y \\ z \end{bmatrix} \qquad B = \begin{bmatrix} 10 \\ 5 \\ -1 \end{bmatrix}
$$

Using matrix multiplication, the system of equations can then be written as $AX = B$. Go through the multiplication to convince yourself that this matrix equation yields the original set of equations.

To simplify the notation, we designate the variables as x_1, x_2, x_3, and so on. Rewriting the initial set of equations using this notation, we have

$$
\begin{array}{rrrcr}
3x_1 & +2x_2 & -x_3 & = & 10 \\
-x_1 & +3x_2 & +2x_3 & = & 5 \\
x_1 & -x_2 & -x_3 & = & -1
\end{array}
$$

This set of equations is then represented by the matrix equation $AX = B$, where X is the column vector $[x_1, x_2, x_3]^T$. We now present two methods for solving a system of N equations with N unknowns.

MATRIX LEFT DIVISION

In MATLAB, a system of simultaneous equations can be solved using matrix left division. Thus, the solution to the matrix equation $AX = B$ is **A\B**. To illustrate, we can define and solve the system of equations in our previous example with these statements:

```
A = [3,2,-1; -1, 3, 2; 1, -1, -1];
B = [10, 5, -1]';
X = A\B;
```

The array **x** is the column vector $[-2, 5, -6]^T$. To confirm that the values of **x** do indeed solve each equation, we can multiply **A** by **x** using the expression **A*x**. The result is the column vector $[10, 5, -1]^T$

If there is not a unique solution to a system of equations, an error message is displayed. The solution vector may contain values of NaN or $+\infty$ or $-\infty$, depending on the values of the matrices **A** and **B**.

MATRIX INVERSE

A system of equations can also be solved using the inverse of a matrix. For example, assume that A, X, and B are the matrices defined earlier:

$$A = \begin{bmatrix} 3 & 2 & -1 \\ -1 & 3 & 2 \\ 1 & -1 & -1 \end{bmatrix} \qquad X = \begin{bmatrix} x_1 \\ x_2 \\ x_3 \end{bmatrix} \qquad B = \begin{bmatrix} 10 \\ 5 \\ -1 \end{bmatrix}$$

Then, $AX = B$. If we premultiply both sides of this matrix equation by A^{-1}, we have $A^{-1}AX = A^{-1}B$. But because $A^{-1}A$ is equal to the identity matrix I, we have $IX = A^{-1}B$, or $X = A^{-1}B$. In MATLAB, we can compute this solution using the following command:

```
X = inv(A)*B;
```

This solution is computed using a different technique than the solution using matrix left division, but both solutions will be the same for a system that is not ill-conditioned.

Practice!

Solve the following systems of equations using both matrix left division and inverse matrices. Use MATLAB to verify that each solution solves the system of equations using matrix multiplication.

1.
$$\begin{aligned} -2x_1 + x_2 &= -3 \\ x_1 + x_2 &= 3 \end{aligned}$$

2.
$$\begin{aligned} 10x_1 - 7x_2 + 0x_3 &= 7 \\ -3x_1 + 2x_2 + 6x_3 &= 4 \\ 5x_1 + x_2 + 5x_3 &= 6 \end{aligned}$$

3.
$$\begin{aligned} x_1 + 4_2 - x_3 + x_4 &= 2 \\ 2x_1 + 7x_2 + x_3 - 2x_4 &= 16 \\ x_1 + 4x_2 - x_3 + 2x_4 &= -15 \\ 3x_1 - 10x_2 - 2x_3 + 5x_4 &= -15 \end{aligned}$$

CHAPTER SUMMARY

In this chapter we defined the transpose, the inverse, and the determinant of a matrix. We also defined the computation of a dot product (between two vectors) and a matrix product (between two matrices). Two methods for solving a system of N equations with N unknowns using matrix operations were presented—one method used matrix left division and the other used the inverse of a matrix.

MATLAB SUMMARY

This MATLAB summary lists all the special characters, commands, and functions that were defined in this chapter. A brief description is also included for each one.

SPECIAL CHARACTERS

'	indicates a matrix transpose
*	indicates matrix multiplication
\	indicates a matrix left division

COMMANDS AND FUNCTIONS

det	computes the determinant of a matrix
inv	computes the inverse of a matrix

PROBLEMS

Single Voltage Source Electrical Circuit. This problem relates to a system of equations generated by the electrical circuit shown in Figure 4.1, which contains a single voltage source and five resistors.

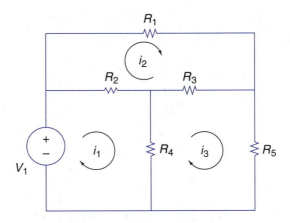

Figure 4.1 *Circuit with one voltage source.*

1. The following set of equations defines the currents in this circuit. Compute the currents using resistor values (R_1, R_2, R_3, R_4) and a voltage value (V_1) entered from the keyboard.

$$
\begin{aligned}
-V_1 \quad +R_2(i_1 - i_2) \quad +R_4(i_1 - i_3) &= 0 \\
R_1 i_2 \quad +R_3(i_2 - i_3) \quad +R_2(i_2 - i_1) &= 0 \\
R_3(i_3 - i_2) \qquad\quad +R_5 i_3 \quad +R_4(i_3 - i_1) &= 0
\end{aligned}
$$

Amino Acids. The amino acids in proteins contain molecules of oxygen(O), carbon(C), nitrogen(N), sulfur(S), and hydrogen(H), as shown in Table 4.1. The molecular weights for oxygen, carbon, nitrogen, sulfur, and hydrogen are

Oxygen	15.9994
Carbon	12.011
Nitrogen	14.00674
Sulfur	32.066
Hydrogen	1.00794

TABLE 4.1 Amino Acid Molecules

Amino Acid	O	C	N	S	H
Alanine	2	3	1	0	7
Arginine	2	6	4	0	15
Asparagine	3	4	2	0	8
Aspartic	4	4	1	0	6
Cysteine	2	3	1	1	7
Glutamic	4	5	1	0	8
Glutamine	3	5	2	0	10
Glycine	2	2	1	0	5
Histidine	2	6	3	0	10
Isoleucine	2	6	1	0	13
Leucine	2	6	1	0	13
Lysine	2	6	2	0	15
Methionine	2	5	1	1	11
Phenylanlanine	2	9	1	0	11
Proline	2	5	1	0	10
Serine	3	3	1	0	7
Threonine	3	4	1	0	9
Tryptophan	2	11	2	0	11
Tyrosine	3	9	1	0	11
Valine	2	5	1	0	11

2. Write a program in which the user enters the number of oxygen atoms, carbon atoms, nitrogen atoms, sulfur atoms, and hydrogen atoms in an amino acid. Compute and print the corresponding molecular weight. Use a dot product to compute the molecular weight.

3. Write a program that computes the molecular weight of each amino acid in Table 4.1, assuming that the numeric information in this table is contained in a data file named `elements.dat`. Generate a new data file named `weights.dat` that contains the molecular weights of the amino acids. Use matrix multiplication to compute the molecular weights.

4. Modify the program developed in problem 3 so that it also computes and prints the average amino acid molecular weight.

5. Modify the program developed in problem 3 so that it also computes and prints the minimum and maximum molecular weights.

5

Courtesy of National Center for Atmospheric Research/ University Corporation for Atmospheric Research/ National Science Foundation.

GRAND CHALLENGE:
Weather Prediction

Weather balloons are used to collect data from the upper atmosphere to use in developing weather models. These balloons are filled with helium and rise to an equilibrium point at which the difference between the densities of the helium inside the balloon and the air outside the balloon is just enough to support the weight of the balloon. During the day, the sun warms the balloon, causing it to rise to a new equilibrium point; in the evening, the balloon cools, and it descends to a lower altitude. The balloon can be used to measure the temperature, pressure, humidity, chemical concentrations, or other properties of the air around the balloon. A weather balloon may stay aloft for only a few hours or as long as several years collecting environmental data. The balloon falls back to earth as the helium leaks out or is released.

Symbolic Mathematics

5.1   Symbolic Algebra

5.2   Equation Solving

5.3   Differentiation and Integration

Chapter Summary, MATLAB Summary, Problems

OBJECTIVES

The previous chapters have demonstrated MATLAB's capabilities for numerical computations. In this chapter, we present some of the capabilities of MATLAB for symbolic manipulations. After showing you how to define a symbolic expression, we discuss the functions for simplifying mathematical expressions and for performing operations on mathematical expressions. In addition, we present sections on solving equations using symbolic mathematics and on performing differentiation and integration using symbolic expressions.

5.1   Symbolic Algebra

Maple V

In the previous chapters we used MATLAB to compute using numbers; in this chapter we use MATLAB to compute using symbols. This capability to manipulate mathematical expressions without using numbers can be very useful in solving certain types of engineering problems. The symbolic functions in MATLAB are based on the **Maple V** software package, which comes from Waterloo Maple Software, Inc., in Canada. A complete set of these symbolic functions is available in the Symbolic Math Toolbox, which is available for the professional version of MATLAB; a subset of the symbolic functions is included with the student edition of MATLAB, Version 4.

Symbolic algebra

In this chapter we focus on **symbolic algebra**, which is used to factor and simplify mathematical expressions, to determine solutions to equations, and to perform integration and differentiation of mathematical expressions. Additional capabilities that we do not discuss in this chapter include linear algebra functions for computing inverses, determinants, eigenvalues, and canonical forms of symbolic matrices; variable precision arithmetic for numerically evaluating mathematical expressions to any specified accuracy; symbolic and numerical solutions to differential equations; and special mathematical functions that evaluate functions such as Fourier transforms. For more details on these additional symbolic capabilities, refer to the second edition of *Engineering Problem Solving with MATLAB* by Delores M. Etter or to the Symbolic Math Toolbox documentation.

SYMBOLIC EXPRESSIONS

A symbolic expression is stored in MATLAB as a character string. Thus, single quote marks are used to define symbolic expressions, as illustrated by the following examples:

```
'tan(y/x)'                  'x^3 - 2*x^2 + 3'
'1/(cos(angle) + 2)'        '3*a*b - 6'
```

Independent variable

In expressions with more than one variable, it is often important to know, or to specify, the **independent variable**. In many functions, the independent variable can be specified as an additional function argument. MATLAB will also select an independent variable that it uses when one is not specified. If there are several variables, MATLAB selects the one that is a single lowercase letter, other than i and j, that is closest to x alphabetically. If there is a tie, the letter later in the alphabet is chosen. If there is no such character, then x is chosen as the independent variable. The function **symvar** will return the independent variable:

```
symvar(s)
```
returns the independent variable for the symbolic expression **s**

The following examples illustrate the use of these rules in determining the independent variable in symbolic expressions:

Expression s	symvar(S)
`'tan(y/x)'`	x
`'x^3 - 2*x^2 + 3'`	x
`'1/(cos(angle) + 2)'`	x
`'3*a*b - 6'`	b

MATLAB includes a function named `ezplot` that generates a plot of a symbolic expression of one variable. The independent variable generally ranges over the interval $[-2\pi, 2\pi]$ unless this interval contains a singularity (a point at which the expression is not defined). A summary of the forms of this function follows:

`ezplot(S)` Generates a plot of **s**, where **s** is assumed to be a function of one variable; the independent variable typically ranges from -2π to 2π.

`ezplot(S,[xmin,xmax])` Generates a plot of **s** where **s** is assumed to be a function of one variable; the independent variable ranges from **xmin** to **xmax**.

SIMPLIFICATION OF MATHEMATICAL EXPRESSIONS

A number of functions are available to simplify mathematical expressions by collecting coefficients, expanding terms, factoring expressions, or just simplifying the expression. A summary of these functions follows:

`collect(S)` Collects coefficients of **s**.

`collect(S,'v')` Collects coefficients of **s** with respect to the independent variable `'v'`.

`expand(S)` Performs an expansion of **s**.

`factor(S)` Returns the factorization of **s**.

`simple(S)` Simplifies the form of **s** to a shorter form if possible.

`simplify(S)` Simplifies **s** using Maple's simplification rules.

To illustrate these functions, assume that the following symbolic expressions have been defined:

```
S1 = 'x^3-1';
S2 = '(x-3)^2+(y-4)^2';
S3 = 'sqrt(a^4*b^7)';
S4 = '14*x^2/(22*x*y);
```

The following list shows function references and their corresponding values:

Reference	Function value
`factor(S1)`	`(x-1)*(x^2+x+1)`
`expand(S2)`	`x^2-6*x+25+y^2-8*y`
`collect(S2)`	`x^2-6*x+9+(y-4)^2`
`collect(S2,'y')`	`y^2 - 8*y + (x-3)^2 + 16`
`simplify(S3)`	`a^2*b^(7/2)`
`simple(S4)`	`7/11*x/y`

OPERATIONS ON SYMBOLIC EXPRESSIONS

The standard arithmetic operations can be applied to symbolic expressions using symbolic functions. Additional symbolic functions can be used to convert a symbolic expression from one form to another. These functions are summarized below:

`horner(S)`	Transposes **s** into its Horner, or nested, representation.
`numden(S)`	Returns two symbolic expressions that represent, respectively, the numerator expression and the denominator expression for the rational representation of **s**.
`numeric(S)`	Converts **s** to a numeric form (**s** must not contain any symbolic variables).
`poly2sym(c)`	Converts a polynomial coefficient vector **c** to a symbolic polynomial.
`pretty(S)`	Prints **s** in an output form that resembles typeset mathematics.
`sym2poly(S)`	Converts **s** to a polynomial coefficient vector.
`symadd(A,B)`	Performs a symbolic addition, **A+B**.
`symdiv(A,B)`	Performs a symbolic division, **A/B**.
`symmul(A,B)`	Performs a symbolic multiplication, **A*B**.
`sympow(S,p)`	Performs a symbolic power, **S^p**.
`symsub(A,B)`	Performs a symbolic subtraction, **A-B**.

To illustrate the use of some of these functions, assume that the following symbolic expressions have been defined:

```
p1 = '1/(y-3)';
p2 = '3*y/(y+2)';
p3 = '(y+4)*(y-3)*y';
```

The following list shows function references and their corresponding values:

Reference	Function value
symmul(p1,p3)	(y+4)*y
sympow(p2,3)	27*y^3/(y+2)^3
symadd(p1,p2)	1/(y-3)+3*y/(y+2)
[num,den]=numden(symadd(p1,p2))	[-8*y+2+3*y^2,(y-3)*(y+2)]
horner(symadd(p3,'1'))	1+(-12+(1+y)*y)*y

Practice!

Use MATLAB to perform the following symbolic operations. Assume the following symbolic expressions have been defined:

```
S1 = '1/(x+4)';
S2 = 'x^2 + 8*x + 16';
S3 = '(x+4)*(x-2)';
```

1. S1/S2
2. S2/(S1^2)
3. S3*S1/S2
4. S2^2

5.2 Equation Solving

Symbolic math functions can be used to solve a single equation, a system of equations, and differential equations. A brief description of the function for solving a single equation or a system of equations follows:

solve(f)	Solves the symbolic equation f for its symbolic variable. Solves the equation f=0 for its symbolic variable if f is a symbolic expression.
solve(f1, . . . fn)	Solves the system of equations represented by f1, . . . , fn.

To illustrate the use of the solve function, assume that the following equations have been defined:

```
eq1 = 'x-3=4';
eq2 = 'x^2-x-6=0';
eq3 = 'x^2+2*x+4=0';
eq4 = '3*x+2*y-z=10';
eq5 = '-x+3*y+2*z=5';
eq6 = 'x-y-z=-1';
```

The following list shows the resulting values from the solve function:

Reference	Function value
solve(eq1)	'7'
solve(eq2)	['3', '-2']'
solve(eq3)	['-1+i*3^(1/2)', '-1-i*3^(1/2)']'
solve(eq4,eq5,eq6)	'x = -2, y = 5, z = -6'

The function for solving ordinary differential equations is **dsolve**, but it is not discussed in this text. For more information on determining the symbolic solution to ordinary differential equations, see the second edition of *Engineering Problem Solving with MATLAB* by Delores M. Etter.

Practice!

Solve the following systems of equations using symbolic mathematics. Compare your answers to those computed using the matrix methods from Chapter 4.

1.
$$\begin{aligned} -2x_1 +x_2 &= -3 \\ x_1 +x_2 &= 3 \end{aligned}$$

2.
$$\begin{aligned} 10x_1 -7x_2 +0x_3 &= 7 \\ -3x_1 +2x_2 +6x_3 &= 4 \\ 5x_1 +x_2 +5x_3 &= 6 \end{aligned}$$

3.
$$\begin{aligned} x_1 \quad 4x_2 -x_3 \quad x_4 &= 2 \\ 2x_1 +7x_2 +x_3 -2x_4 &= 16 \\ x_1 +4x_2 -x3 \quad 2x_4 &= 1 \\ 3x_1 -10x_2 -2x_3 +5x_4 &= -15 \end{aligned}$$

5.3   Differentiation and Integration

The operations of differentiation and integration are used extensively in solving engineering problems. In this section we discuss the differentiation and integration of symbolic expressions. In the next chapter we discuss techniques for performing numerical differentiation and numerical integration using data values instead of symbolic expressions.

DIFFERENTIATION

The **diff** function is used to determine the symbolic derivative of a symbolic expression. There are four forms in which the **diff** function can be used to perform symbolic differentiation:

diff(f)	Returns the derivative of the expression **f** with respect to the default independent variable.
diff(f,'t')	Returns the derivative of the expression **f** with respect to the variable **t**.
diff(f,n)	Returns the **n**th derivative of the expression **f** with respect to the default independent variable.
diff(f,'t',n)	Returns the **n**th derivative of the expression **f** with respect to the variable **t**.

We now present several examples using the **diff** function for symbolic differentiation. Assume that the following expressions have been defined:

```
S1 = '6*x^3-4*x^2+b*x-5';
S2 = 'sin(a)';
S3 = '(1 - t^3)/(1 + t^4)';
```

The following list shows function references and their corresponding values:

Reference	Function value
diff(S1)	**18*x^2-8*x+b**
diff(S1,2)	**36*x-8**
diff(S1,'b')	**x**
diff(S2)	**cos(a)**
diff(S3)	**-3*t^2/(1+t^4)-4*(1-t^3)/(1+t^4)^2*t^3**
simplify(diff(S3))	**t^2*(-3+t^4-4*t)/(1+t^4)^2**

Practice!

Determine the first and second derivatives of the following functions using MATLAB's symbolic functions.

1. $g(x) = x^3 - 5x^2 + 2x + 8$
2. $g_2(x) = (x^2 + 4x + 4)*(x - 1)$
3. $g_3(x) = (x^2 - 2x + 2)/(10x - 24)$
4. $g_4(x) = (x^5 - 4x^4 - 9x^3 + 32)^2$

INTEGRATION

The **int** function is used to integrate a symbolic expression **f**. This function attempts to find the symbolic expression **F** such that **diff(F) = f**. It is possible that the integral (or antiderivative) may not exist in closed form or that MATLAB cannot find the integral. In these cases, the function will return the command unevaluated. The **int** function can be used in the following forms:

int(f)	Returns the integral of the expression **f** with respect to the default independent variable.
int(f,'t')	Returns the integral of the expression **f** with respect to the variable **t**.
int(f,a,b)	Returns the integral of the expression **f** with respect to the default independent variable evaluated over the interval [**a,b**], where **a** and **b** are numeric expressions.
int(f,'t',a,b)	Returns the integral of the expression **f** with respect to the variable **t** evaluated over the interval [**a,b**], where **a** and **b** are numeric expressions.
int(f,'m','n')	Returns the integral of the expression **f** with respect to the default independent variable evaluated over the interval [**m,n**], where **m** and **n** are symbolic expressions.

We now present several examples using the **int** function for symbolic integration. Assume that the following expressions have been defined:

```
S1 = '6*x^3-4*x^2+b*x-5';
S2 = 'sin(a)';
S3 = 'sqrt(x)';
```

The following list shows function references and their corresponding values:

Reference	Function value
int(S1)	3/2*x^4-4/3*x^3+1/2*b*x^2-5*x
int(S2)	-cos(a)
int(S3)	2/3*x^(3/2)
int(S3,'a','b')	2/3*b^(3/2) - 2/3*a^(3/2)
int(S3,0.5,0.6)	2/25*15^(1/2)-1/6*2^(1/2)
numeric(int(S3,0.5,0.6))	0.0741

Practice!

Use MATLAB's symbolic functions to determine the values of the following integrals.

1. $\displaystyle\int_{0.5}^{0.6} |x|\,dx$

2. $$\int_{0}^{1} |x|\,dx$$

3. $$\int_{-1}^{-0.5} |x|\,dx$$

4. $$\int_{-0.5}^{0.5} |x|\,dx$$

CHAPTER SUMMARY

In this chapter we presented MATLAB's functions for performing symbolic mathematics. Examples were given to illustrate simplification of expressions, operations with symbolic expressions, and deriving symbolic solutions to equations. In addition, we presented the MATLAB functions for determining the symbolic derivatives and integrals of expressions.

MATLAB SUMMARY

This MATLAB summary lists all the special characters, commands, and functions that were defined in this chapter. A brief description is also included for each one.

SPECIAL CHARACTER

'   used to enclose a symbolic expression

COMMANDS AND FUNCTIONS

collect	collects coefficients of a symbolic expression
diff	differentiates a symbolic expression
expand	expands a symbolic expression
ezplot	generates a plot of a symbolic expression
factor	factors a symbolic expression
horner	converts a symbolic expression into a nested form
int	integrates a symbolic expression
numden	returns the numerator and denominator expressions
numeric	converts a string to a number
poly2sym	converts a vector to a symbolic polynomial

pretty	prints a symbolic expression in typeset form
simple	shortens a symbolic expression
simplify	simplifies a symbolic expression
solve	solves an equation
sym2poly	converts a symbolic expression to a coefficient vector
symadd	adds two symbolic expressions
symdiv	divides two symbolic expressions
symmul	multiplies two symbolic expressions
sympow	raises a symbolic expression to a power
symsub	subtracts two symbolic expressions
symvar	returns independent variable

PROBLEMS

Weather Balloons. Assume that the following polynomial represents the altitude in meters during the first 48 hours following the launch of a weather balloon:

$$h(t) = -0.12t^4 + 12t^3 - 380t^2 + 4100t + 220$$

Assume that the units of t are hours.

1. Use MATLAB to determine the equation for the velocity of the weather balloon, using the fact that the velocity is the derivative of the altitude.
2. Use MATLAB to determine the equation for the acceleration of the weather balloon. Compare results from using the facts that the acceleration is the second derivative of the altitude and that the acceleration is the derivative of the velocity (see problem 1).
3. Use your answers to problems 1 and 2 to generate plots of the altitude, velocity, and acceleration for the interval 0 to 48 hours.

Water Flow. Assume that water is pumped into an initially empty tank. It is known that the rate of flow of water into the tank at time t (in seconds) is 50-t liters per second. The amount of water Q that flows into the tank during the first x seconds can be shown to be equal to the integral of the expression (50-t) evaluated from 0 to x seconds.

4. Determine a symbolic equation that represents the amount of water in the tank after x seconds.
5. Determine the amount of water in the tank after 30 seconds.
6. Determine the amount of water that flowed into the tank between 10 seconds and 15 seconds after the flow was initiated.

Elastic Spring. Consider a spring with the left end held fixed and the right end free to move along the x axis. We assume that the right end of the spring is at the origin $x = 0$ when the spring is at rest. When the spring is stretched, the right end of the spring is at some new value of x that is greater than zero. When the spring is compressed, the right end of the spring is at some value of x that is less than zero. Assume that a spring has a natural length of 1 ft and that a force of 10 lbs is required to compress the spring to a length of 0.5 ft. It can then be shown that the work (in ft/lb) done to stretch this spring from its natural length to a total length of n ft is equal to the integral of $20x$ over the interval from 0 to $n-1$.

7. Use MATLAB to determine a symbolic expression that represents the amount of work necessary to stretch the spring to a total length of n ft.

8. What is the amount of work done to stretch this spring to a total of 2 feet.

9. If the amount of work exerted is 25 ft/lb, what is the length of the stretched spring?

6

Courtesy of Chevron Corporation.

GRAND CHALLENGE:
Enhanced Oil and Gas Recovery

The design and construction of the Alaska pipeline presented numerous engineering challenges. One of the most important problems that had to be addressed was protecting the permafrost (the perennially frozen subsoil in arctic or subarctic regions) from the heat of the pipeline itself. The oil flowing in the pipeline is warmed by pumping stations and by friction from the walls of the pipe, enough so that the supports holding the pipeline have to be insulated or even cooled to keep them from melting the permafrost at their bases.

Numerical Techniques

OBJECTIVES

In this chapter we present several important numerical techniques used frequently to solve engineering problems. Interpolation and curve-fitting techniques are used to approximate new data points, using a set of data points collected from an experiment or from observing a physical phenomena. Numerical integration and differentiation techniques are used to provide approximations to integrals and derivatives of functions, using data points from the functions.

6.1   Interpolation

In this section we present two types of interpolation—linear interpolation and cubic-spline interpolation. In both techniques, we assume that we have a set of data points that represent a set of xy coordinates for which y is a function of x; that is, $y = f(x)$. We further assume that we need to estimate a value $f(b)$, which is not one of the original data points, but for which b is between two of the x values from the original set of data points. We want to approximate (or interpolate) a value for $f(b)$, using the information from the original set of data points. In Figure 6.1, we show a set of six data points that have been connected with straight line segments and that have also been connected with cubic degree polynomial segments. From this figure, we see that the values determined for the function between sample points depend on the type of interpolation that we select.

LINEAR INTERPOLATION

**Linear
interpolation**

Linear interpolation is one of the most common techniques for estimating data between two given data points. If we assume that the function between the two

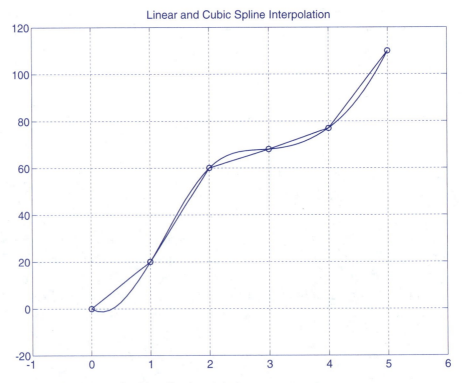

Figure 6.1 *Linear and cubic-spline interpolation.*

points can be estimated by a straight line drawn between the two data values, we can compute the function value at any point between the two data values, using an equation derived from similar triangles.

CUBIC-SPLINE INTERPOLATION

Cubic spline   A **cubic spline** is a smooth curve constructed to go through a set of points. The curve between each pair of points is a third-degree polynomial (which has the general form of $a_0x^3 + a_1x^2 + a_2x + a_3$) that is computed so that it provides a smooth curve between the two points and a smooth transition from the third-degree polynomial between the previous pair of points. Refer to the cubic spline shown in Figure 6.1 that connects six points. A total of five different cubic equations are used to generate this smooth function that joins all six points.

interp1 FUNCTION

The MATLAB function that performs interpolation has three forms. Each form assumes that vectors **x** and **y** contains the original data values and that another vector **x_new** contains the new points for which we want to compute interpolated **y_new** values. (The **x** values should be in ascending order, and the **x_new** values should be within the range of the **x** values.) A summary of these forms is as follows:

interp1(x,y,x_new)	Returns a vector the size of **x_new** that contains the interpolated *y* values that correspond to **x_new** using linear interpolation.
interp1(x,y,x_new,'linear')	Returns a vector the size of **x_new** that contains the interpolated *y* values that correspond to **x_new** using linear interpolation.
interp1(x,y,x_new,'spline')	Returns a vector the size of **x_new** that contains the interpolated *y* values that correspond to **x_new** using cubic-spline interpolation.

The statements that performed the interpolation and plotted the functions in Figure 6.1 are the following:

```
%  These statements compare linear interpolation
%  with cubic spline interpolation. (Figure 6.1)
%
x = 0:5;
y = [0,20,60,68,77,110];
newx = 0:0.1:5;
newy_1 = interp1(x,y,newx,'linear');
newy_2 = interp1(x,y,newx,'spline');
```

```
plot(newx,newy_1,newx,newy_2,x,y,'o'),
title('Linear and Cubic Spline Interpolation'),grid,
axis([-1,6,-20,120]),pause
```

Practice!

Assume that we have the following set of data points:

Time, s	Temperature, °F
0.0	72.5
0.5	78.1
1.0	86.4
1.5	92.3
2.0	110.6
2.5	111.5
3.0	109.3
3.5	110.2
4.0	110.5
4.5	109.9
5.0	110.2

1. Generate a plot to compare connecting the temperature points with straight lines and with cubic splines.

2. Compare temperature values at these times, using linear interpolation and cubic-spline interpolation:

    0.3,   1.25,   2.36,   4.48

3. Compute time values that correspond to these temperatures, using linear interpolation and cubic-spline interpolation:

    81,   96,   100,   106

6.2   Curve Fitting

Least-squares

Assume that we have a set of data points collected from an experiment. After plotting the data points, we find that they generally fall in a straight line. However, if we try to draw a straight line through points, only a couple of the points would probably fall exactly on the line. A **least-squares** curve-fitting method could be used to find the straight line that was the closest to the points by minimizing the distance from each point to the straight line. Although this line can be considered a "best fit" to the data points, it is possible that none of the points would actually fall on the best fit line. (Note that this is very different from inter-polation because the curves used in linear interpolation and cubic-spline interpo-lation actually contained all the original data points.) In this section we first present a discussion on fitting a straight line to a set of data points, and then we discuss fitting a polynomial to a set of data points.

LINEAR REGRESSION

Linear regression   **Linear regression** is the name given to the process that determines the linear equation that is the best fit to a set of data points in terms of minimizing the sum of the squared distances between the line and the data points. To understand this process, we first consider the set of data values used in the interpolation discus-sion from the previous section. If we plot these points, it appears that a good esti-mate of a line through the points is $y = 20x$, as shown in Figure 6.2. The follow-ing commands were used to generate this plot:

```
%  These statements compare a linear model
%  to a set of data points. (Figure 6.2)
%
x = 0:5;
y = [0,20,60,68,77,110];
y1 = 20*x;
plot(x,y1,x,y,'o'),title('Linear Estimate'),
xlabel('Time, s'),ylabel('Temperature, Degrees F'),grid,
axis([-1,6,-20,120]),pause
```

To measure the quality of the fit of this linear estimate to the data, we first de-termine the distance from each point to the linear estimate; these distances are also shown in Figure 6.2. The first two points fall exactly on the line, so d_1 and d_2 are zero. The value of d_3 is equal to $60 - 40$, or 20; the rest of the distances can be com-puted in a similar way. If we compute the sum of the distances, some of the positive and negative values would cancel each other and give a sum that is smaller than it should be. To avoid this problem, we could add absolute values or squared values; linear regression uses squared values. Therefore, the measure of the quality of the fit of this linear estimate is the sum of the **squared distances** between the points and the linear estimates. This sum can be computed with the following command:

Squared distances

```
sum_sq = sum((y-y1).^2)
```

For this set of data, the value of **sum_sq** is 573.

If we drew another line through the points, we could compute the sum of squares that corresponds to this new line. Of the two lines, the better fit is pro-vided by the line with the smaller sum of squared distances. To find the line with the smallest sum of squared distances, we can write an equation that computes the distances using a general linear equation $y = mx + b$. We then write an equa-tion that represents the sum of the squared distances; this equation will have m and b as its variables. Using techniques from calculus, we can then compute the

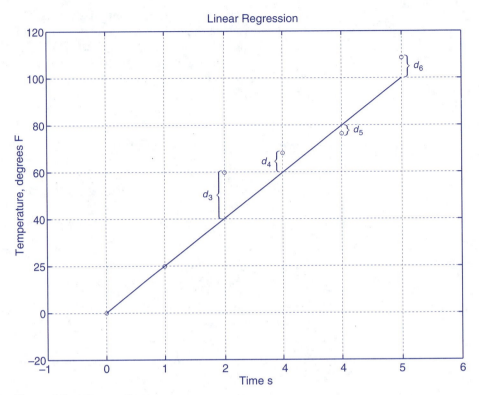

Figure 6.2 *A linear estimate.*

derivatives of the equation with respect to m and b and set the derivatives equal to zero. The values of m and b that are determined in this way represent the straight line with the minimum sum of squared distances. The MATLAB statement for computing this best-fit linear equation is discussed in the next section. For the data presented in this section, the best fit is shown in Figure 6.3; the corresponding sum of squares is 356.8190.

POLYNOMIAL REGRESSION

In the previous discussion we presented a technique for computing the linear equation that best fits a set of data. A similar technique can be developed using a single polynomial (not a set of polynomials as in a cubic spline) to fit the data by minimizing the distance of the polynomial from the data points. First, recall that a polynomial with one variable can be written in the following general formula:

$$f(x) = a_0 x^n + a_1 x^{n-1} + a_2 x^{n-2} + \ldots + a_{n-1} x + a_n$$

Degree   The **degree** of a polynomial is equal to the largest value used as an exponent. Therefore, the general form for a cubic polynomial is

$$g(x) = a_0 x^3 + a_1 x^2 + a_2 x + a_3$$

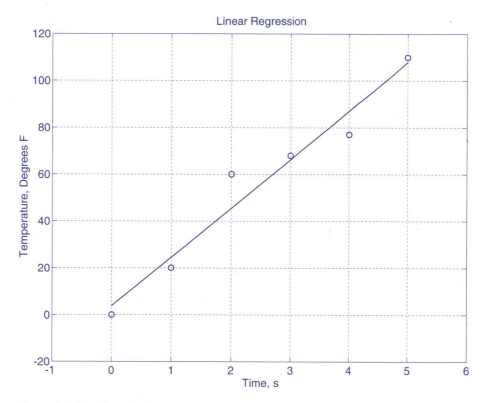

Figure 6.3 *Best-fit estimate.*

Note that a linear equation is also a polynomial of degree one.

In Figure 6.4 we plot the original set of data points that we used in the linear regression example, along with plots of the best-fit polynomials with degrees 2 through 5. Note that as the degree of the polynomial increases, the number of points that fall on the curve also increases. If a set of n points is used to determine an nth-degree polynomial, all n points will fall on the polynomial.

polyfit AND polyval FUNCTIONS

The MATLAB function for computing the best fit to a set of data with a polynomial with a specified degree is the **polyfit** function. This function has three arguments—the x and y coordinates of the data points and the degree n of the polynomial. The function returns the coefficients, in descending powers of x, of the nth degree polynomial that fits the vectors x and y. (Note that there are $n + 1$ coefficients for an nth degree polynomial.) A summary of this function is

polyfit(x,y,n)	Returns a vector of **n+1** coefficients that represents the best-fit polynomial of degree **n** for the x and y coordinates. The coefficient order corresponds to decreasing powers of x.

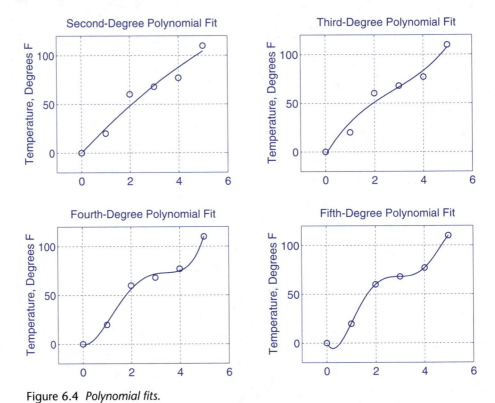

Figure 6.4 *Polynomial fits.*

The best linear fit for the example data, plotted in Figure 6.3, and its corresponding least-squares sum are determined with these statements:

```
%  These statements compute a best-fit linear mode.
%  for a set of data points. (Figure 6.3)
%
x = 0:5;
y = [0,20,60,68,77,110];
coef = polyfit(x,y,1);
m = coef(1);
b = coef(2);
ybest = m*x + b;
sum_sq = sum((y - ybest).^2);
plot(x,ybest,x,y,'o'),title('Linear Regression'),
xlabel('Time, s'),ylabel('Temperature, Degrees F'),grid,
axis([-1,6,-20,120]),pause
```

The **polyval** function is used to evaluate a polynomial at a set of data points. The first argument of the **polyval** function is a vector containing the coefficients of the polynomial (in an order corresponding to decreasing powers of *x*), and the second argument is the vector of **x** values for which we want polynomial values. A summary of this function is

polyval(coef,x)   Returns a vector of polynomial values *f(x)* that corre-
                         spond to the **x** vector values. The order of the coeffi-
                         cients corresponds to decreasing powers of *x*.

In the previous example, we computed the points of the linear regression using values from the coefficients. We could also have computed them using the **polyval** function as shown here:

```
ybest = polyval(coef,x);
```

Using the same data that was used for the linear regression example, we can now illustrate the computation of the best-fit polynomials of degree 2 through degree 5 that were shown in Figure 6.4:

```
%  These statements compute polynomial models
%  for a set of data points. (Figure 6.4)
%
x = 0:5;
y = [0,20,60,68,77,110];
newx = 0:0.05:5;
for n=1:4
    f(:,n) = polyval(polyfit(x,y,n+1),newx)';
end
```

Then, for example, to plot the second-degree polynomial, we could use this statement:

```
plot(newx,f(:,1),x,y,'o')
```

Additional statements are necessary to define the subplot, label each plot, and set the axes limits. From the previous discussion on polynomial fits, we would expect that the lower degree polynomials would not contain all data points, but that the fifth degree polynomial would contain all six data points; the plots in Figure 6.4 verify these expectations.

6.3   Numerical Integration

The integral of a function *f(x)* over the interval [*a,b*] is defined to be the area under the curve of *f(x)* between *a* and *b*, as shown in Figure 6.5. If the value of this integral is *K*, the notation to represent this integral of *f(x)* between *a* and *b* is

$$K = \int_a^b f(x)dx$$

For many functions, this integral can be computed analytically. However, for a number of functions, this integral cannot easily be computed analytically, and thus requires a numerical technique to estimate its value. The numerical evaluation

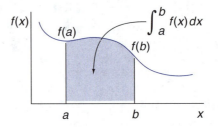

Figure 6.5 *Integral of f(x) from a to b.*

Quadrature

of an integral is also called **quadrature**, which comes from an ancient geometrical problem.

The numerical integration techniques estimate the function $f(x)$ by another function $g(x)$, where $g(x)$ is chosen so that we can easily compute the area under $g(x)$. Then, the better the estimate of $g(x)$ to $f(x)$, the better will be the estimate of the integral of $f(x)$. Two of the most common numerical integration techniques estimate $f(x)$ with a set of piecewise linear functions or with a set of piecewise parabolic functions. If we estimate the function with piecewise linear functions, we can then compute the area of the trapezoids that compose the area under the piecewise linear functions; this technique is called the trapezoidal rule. If we estimate the function with piecewise quadratic functions, we can then compute and add the areas of these components; this technique is called Simpson's rule.

TRAPEZOIDAL RULE AND SIMPSON'S RULE

Trapezoidal rule

If the area under a curve is represented by trapezoids and if the interval $[a,b]$ is divided into n equal sections, then the area can be approximated by the following formula (**trapezoidal rule**):

$$K_T = \frac{b-a}{2n}(f(x_0) + 2f(x_1) + 2f(x_2) + \ldots + 2f(x_{n-1}) + f(x_n))$$

where the x_i values represent the endpoints of the trapezoids and where $x_0 = a$ and $x_n = b$.

Simpson's rule

If the area under a curve is represented by areas under quadratic sections of a curve and if the interval $[a,b]$ is divided into $2n$ equal sections, then the area can be approximated by the following formula (**Simpson's rule**):

$$K_S = \frac{h}{3}(f(x_0) + 4f(x_1) + 2f(x_2) + 4f(x_3) + \ldots 2f(x_{2n-2}) + 4f(x_{2n-1}) + f(x_{2n}))$$

where the x_i values represent the endpoints of the sections and where $x_0 = a$ and $x_{2n} = b$, and $h = (b-a)/(2n)$.

If the piecewise components of the approximating function are higher-degree functions (trapezoidal rule uses linear functions and Simpson's rule uses quadratic functions), the integration techniques are referred to as Newton-Cotes integration techniques.

The estimate of an integral improves as we use more components (such as trapezoids) to approximate the area under a curve. If we attempt to integrate a function with a singularity (a point at which the function or its derivatives are infinity or are not defined), we may not be able to get a satisfactory answer with a numerical integration technique.

MATLAB QUADRATURE FUNCTIONS

MATLAB has two quadrature functions for performing numerical function integration. The **quad** function uses an adaptive form of Simpson's rule, whereas **quad8** uses an adaptive Newton-Cotes 8-panel rule. The **quad8** function is better at handling functions with certain types of singularities, such as $\int_0^1 \sqrt{x}\,dx$. Both functions print a warning message if they detect a singularity, but an estimate of the integral is still returned.

The simplest form of the **quad** and **quad8** functions requires three arguments. The first argument is the name (in quote marks) of the MATLAB function that returns a vector of values of $f(x)$ when given a vector of input values **x**. This function name can be the name of another MATLAB function, such as **sin**, or it can be the name of a user-written MATLAB function. The second and third arguments are the integral limits **a** and **b**. A summary of these functions is

quad('function',a,b)   Returns the area of the **'function'** between **a** and **b**, assuming that **'function'** is a MATLAB function.

quad8('function',a,b)   Returns the area of the **'function'** between **a** and **b**, assuming that **'function'** is a MATLAB function.

These integration techniques can handle some singularities that occur at one or the other interval endpoints, but they cannot handle singularities that occur within the interval. For these cases, you should consider dividing the interval into subintervals and providing estimates of the singularities using other results such as l'Hôpital's Rule.

To illustrate, assume that we want to determine the integral of the square root function for non-negative values of a and b:

$$K_Q = \int_a^b \sqrt{x}\,dx$$

The square root function $f(x) = \sqrt{x}$ is plotted in Figure 6.6 for the interval [0, 5]; the function values are complex for $x < 0$. This function can be integrated analytically to yield the following for non-negative values of a and b:

$$K = \frac{2}{3}(b^{3/2} - a^{3/2})$$

To compare the results of the **quad** and **quad8** functions with the analytical results for a user-specified interval, we use the following statements:

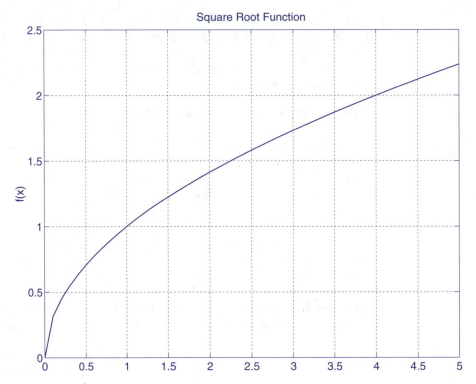

Figure 6.6 *Square root function.*

```
%  These statements compare the quad and quad8 functions with the
%  analytical results for the integration of the square root of x
%  over an interval [a,b], where a and b are non-negative.
%
a = input('Enter left endpoint (non-negative): ' );
b = input('Enter right endpoint (non-negative): ' );
k = 2/3*(b^(1.5) - a^(1.5));
kq = quad('sqrt',a,b);
kq8 = quad8('sqrt',a,b);
fprintf('Analytical: %f \n Numerical: %f %f \n',k,kq,kq8)
```

These statements were tested using several intervals, giving the following results:

Interval [0.5,0.6]

```
        Analytical: 0.074136
        Numerical: 0.074136 0.074136
```

Interval [0,0.5]

```
        Analytical: 0.235702
        Numerical: 0.235701 0.235702
```

Interval [0,1]

Analytical: 0.666667
Numerical: 0.666663 0.666667

The **quad** and **quad8** functions can also include a fourth argument that represents a tolerance. The integration function continues to refine its estimate for the integration until the relative error is less than the tolerance:

$$\frac{\text{previous estimate} - \text{current estimate}}{\text{previous estimate}} < \text{tolerance}$$

If the tolerance is omitted, a default value of 0.001 is assumed.

Practice!

Sketch the function $f(x) = |x|$, and indicate the areas specified by the following integrals. Then compute the integrals by hand, and compare your results to those generated by the **quad** function.

1. $$\int_{0.5}^{0.6} |x|dx$$

2. $$\int_{0}^{1} |x|dx$$

3. $$\int_{-1}^{-0.5} |x|dx$$

4. $$\int_{-0.5}^{0.5} |x|dx$$

6.4   Numerical Differentiation

The derivative of a function $f(x)$ is defined to be a function $f'(x)$ that is equal to the rate of change of $f(x)$ with respect to x. The derivative can be expressed as a ratio, with the change in $f(x)$ indicated by $df(x)$ and the change in x indicated by dx, giving

$$f'(x) = \frac{df(x)}{dx}$$

There are many physical processes in which we want to measure the rate of change of a variable. For example, velocity is the rate of change of position (as in meters per second), and acceleration is the rate of change of velocity (as in meters per second squared). It can also be shown that the integral of acceleration is velocity and that the integral of velocity is position. Hence, integration and differentiation have a special relationship in that they can be considered to be inverses of each other—the integral of a derivative returns the original function, and the derivative of an integral returns the original function, to within a constant value.

The derivative $f'(x)$ can be described graphically as the slope of the function $f(x)$, where the slope of $f(x)$ is defined to be the slope of the tangent line to the function at the specified point. Thus, the value of $f'(x)$ at the point a is $f'(a)$, and it is equal to the slope of the tangent line at the point a, as shown in Figure 6.7.

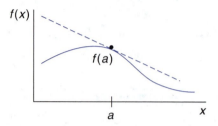

Figure 6.7 *Derivative of f(x) at x = a.*

Critical points

Because the derivative of a function at a point is the slope of the tangent line at the point, a value of zero for the derivative of a function at the point x_k indicates that the line is horizontal at that point. Points with derivatives of zero are called **critical points** and can represent either a horizontal region of the function or a local maximum or a local minimum of the function. (The point may also be the global maximum or global minimum as shown in Figure 6.8, but more analysis of the entire function would be needed to determine this.) If we evaluate the derivative of a function at several points in an interval and we observe that the sign of the derivative changes, then a local maximum or a local minimum occurs in the interval. The second derivative (the derivative of $f'(x)$) can be used to determine whether or not the critical points represent local maxima or local minima. More specifically, if the

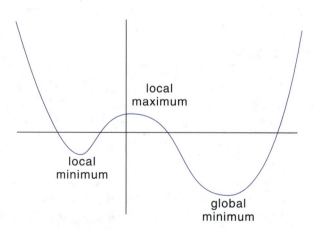

Figure 6.8 *Example of function with critical points.*

Extreme point

second derivative of an **extrema point** is positive, then the function value at the extrema point is a local minimum; if the second derivative of an extrema point is negative, then the function value at the extrema point is a local maximum.

DIFFERENCE EXPRESSIONS

Numerical differentiation techniques estimate the derivative of a function at a point x_k by approximating the slope of the tangent line at x_k using values of the function at points near x_k. The approximation of the slope of the tangent line can be done in several ways, as shown in Figure 6.9.

Figure 6.9(a) assumes that the derivative at x_k is estimated by computing the slope of the line between $f(x_{k-1})$ and $f(x_k)$, as in

$$f'(x_k) = \frac{f(x_k) - f(x_{k-1})}{x_k - x_{k-1}}$$

Backward difference

This type of derivative approximation is called a **backward difference** approximation.

Figure 6.9(b) assumes that the derivative at x_k is estimated by computing the slope of the line between $f(x_k)$ and $f(x_{k+1})$, as in

$$f'(x_k) = \frac{f(x_{k+1}) - f(x_k)}{x_{k+1} - x_k}$$

Forward difference

This type of derivative approximation is called a **forward difference** approximation.

Figure 6.9(c) assumes that the derivative at x_k is estimated by computing the slope of the line between $f(x_{k-1})$ and $f(x_{k+1})$, as in

$$f'(x_k) = \frac{f(x_{k+1}) - f(x_{k-1})}{x_{k+1} - x_{k-1}}$$

Central difference

This type of derivative approximation is called a **central difference** approximation, and we usually assume that x_k is halfway between x_{k-1} and x_{k+1}. The

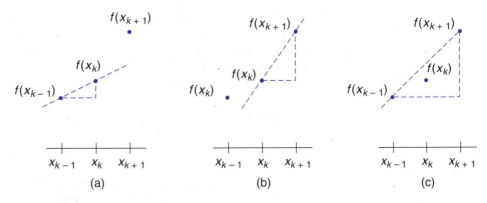

Figure 6.9 *Techniques for computing $f'(x_k)$.*

quality of all of these types of derivative computations depends on the distance between the points used to estimate the derivative; the estimate of the derivative improves as the distance between the two points decreases.

The second derivative of a function $f(x)$ is the derivative of the first derivative of the function

$$f''(x) = \frac{df'(x)}{dx}$$

This function can be evaluated using slopes of the first derivative. Thus, if we use backward differences, we have

$$f''(x_k) = \frac{f'(x_k) - f'(x_{k-1})}{x_k - x_{k-1}}$$

Similar expressions can be derived for computing estimates of higher derivatives.

diff FUNCTION

The **diff** function computes differences between adjacent values in a vector, generating a new vector with one less value. If the **diff** function is applied to a matrix, it operates on the columns of the matrix as if each column were a vector. Thus, the matrix returned has the same number of columns, but one fewer rows. A summary of this function is

> **diff(x)**   Returns a new vector containing differences between adjacent values in the vector **x**. Returns a matrix containing differences between adjacent values in the columns if **x** is a matrix.

To illustrate, assume that the vector **x** contains the values [0,1,2,3,4,5] and the vector y contains the values [2,3,1,5,8,10]. Then the vector generated by **diff(x)** is [1,1,1,1,1], and the vector generated by **diff(y)** is [1,-2,4,3,2]. The derivative **dy** is computed with **diff(y)./diff(x)**. Note that these values of **dy** are correct for both the forward difference equation and the backward difference equation. The distinction between the two methods for computing the derivative is determined by the values of **xd**, which correspond to the derivative **dy**. If the corresponding values of **xd** are [1,2,3,4,5], **dy** computes a backward difference; if the corresponding values of **xd** are [0,1,2,3,4], **dy** computes a forward difference.

Suppose that we have a function given by the following polynomial:

$$f(x) = x^5 - 3x^4 - 11x^3 + 27x^2 + 10x - 24$$

A plot of this function is shown in Figure 6.10. Assume that we want to compute the derivative of this function over the interval $[-4,5]$, using a backward differ-

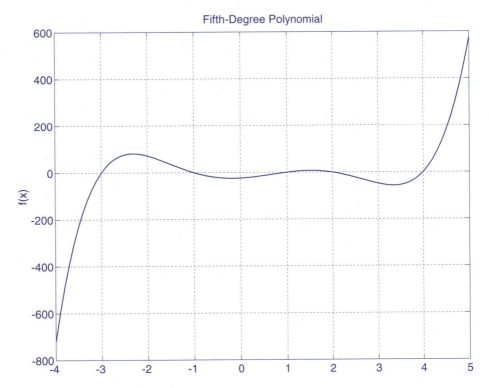

Figure 6.10 *Plot of a polynomial.*

ence equation. We can perform this operation using the **diff** function as shown in these equations, where **df** represents $f'(x)$ and **xd** represents the **x** values corresponding to the derivative:

```
%  Evaluate f(x) and f'(x).
%
x = -4:0.1:5;
f = x.^5 - 3*x.^4 - 11*x.^3 + 27*x.^2 + 10*x - 24;
df = diff(f)./diff(x);
xd = x(2:length(x));
```

Figure 6.11 contains a plot of this derivative. Note that the zeros of the derivative correspond to the points of local minima or local maxima of this function. This function does not have a global minimum or a global maximum because the function ranges from $-\infty$ to $+\infty$. We can print the locations of the critical points (which occur at -2.3, -0.2, 1.5, and 3.4) for this function with the following statements:

```
%  Find locations of critical points of f'(x).
%
product = df(1:length(df)-1).*df(2:length(df));
critical = xd(find(product<0))
```

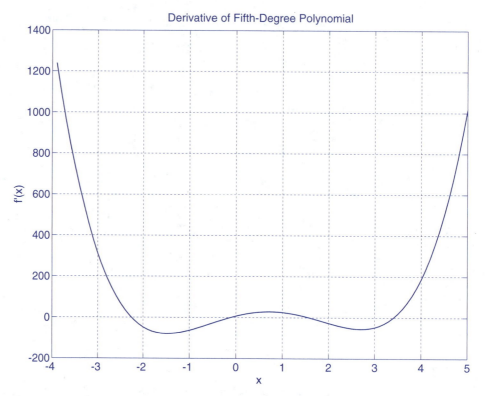

Figure 6.11 *Plot of the derivative of a polynomial.*

The **find** function determines the indices **k** of the locations in **product** for which **df(k)** is equal to 0. These indices are then used with the **xd** vector to print the approximation to the locations of the critical points.

To compute a central difference derivative using the **x** and **f** vectors, we could use the following statements:

```
% Evaluate f'(x) using central differences.
%
numerator = f(3:length(f)) - f(1:length(f)-2);
denominator = x(3:length(x)) - x(1:length(x)-2);
dy = numerator./denominator;
xd = x(2:length(x)-1);
```

In the example discussed in this section, we assumed that we had the equation of the function to be differentiated, and thus we could generate points of the function. In many engineering problems, the data to be differentiated are collected from experiments. Thus, we cannot choose the points to be close together to get a more accurate measure of the derivative. In these cases, it might be a good solution to use the techniques from Section 6.2 that allow us to determine an equation for a polynomial that fits a set of data and then compute points from the equation to use in computing values of the derivative.

Practice!

For each of the following, plot the function, its first derivative, and its second derivative over the interval [-10,10]. Then use MATLAB commands to print the locations of the local minima.

1. $g_1(x) = x^3 - 5x^2 + 2x + 8$
2. $g_2(x) = x^2 + 4x + 4$
3. $g_3(x) = x^2 - 2x + 2$
4. $g_4(x) = 10x - 24$
5. $g_5(x) = x^5 - 4x^4 - 9x^3 + 32x^2 + 28x - 48$

CHAPTER SUMMARY

In this chapter we explained the difference between interpolation and least-squares curve fitting. Two types of interpolation were presented—linear interpolation and cubic-spline interpolation. After presenting the MATLAB commands for performing these types of interpolations, we then turned to least-squares curve fitting using polynomials. This discussion included determining the best fit to a set of data using a polynomial with a specified degree and then using the best-fit polynomial to generate new values of the function. Techniques for numerical integration and differentiation were also presented in this chapter. Numerical integration techniques approximate the area under a curve, and numerical differentiation techniques approximate the slope of a curve. The functions for integration are **quad** and **quad8**. The function used to compute the derivative of a function is the **diff** function, which computes differences between adjacent elements of a vector.

MATLAB SUMMARY

This MATLAB summary lists all commands and functions that were defined in this chapter. A brief description is also included for each one.

COMMANDS AND FUNCTIONS

diff	computes the differences between adjacent values
interp1	computes linear and cubic interpolation
polyfit	computes a least-squares polynomial
polyval	evaluates a polynomial
quad	computes the integral under a curve (Simpson)
quad8	computes the integral under a curve (Newton-Cote)

PROBLEMS

Cylinder Head Temperatures. Assume that the following set of temperature measurements is taken from the cylinder head in a new engine that is being tested for possible use in a race car:

Time, s	Temperature, °F
0.0	0.0
1.0	20.0
2.0	60.0
3.0	68.0
4.0	77.0
5.0	110.0

1. Compare plots of these data, assuming linear interpolation and assuming cubic interpolation for values between the data points, using time values from 0 to 5 in increments of 0.1 s.

2. Using the data from problem 1, find the time value for which there is the largest difference between its linear interpolated temperature and its cubic interpolated temperature.

3. Assume that we measure temperatures at three points around the cylinder head in the engine, instead of at just one point. The set of data is then the following:

Time, s	Temp1	Temp2	Temp3
0.0	0.0	0.0	0.0
1.0	20.0	25.0	52.0
2.0	60.0	62.0	90.0
3.0	68.0	67.0	91.0
4.0	77.0	82.0	93.0
5.0	110.0	103.0	96.0

Assume that these data have been stored in a matrix with six rows and four columns. Determine interpolated values of temperature at the three points in the engine at 2.6 seconds, using linear interpolation.

4. Using the information from problem 3, determine the time that the temperature reached 75 degrees at each of the three points in the cylinder head.

Spacecraft Accelerometer. The guidance and control system for a spacecraft often utilizes a sensor called an accelerometer, which is an electromechanical device that produces an output voltage proportional to the applied acceleration. Assume that an experiment has yielded the following data:

Acceleration	Voltage
−4	−0.593
−2	−0.436
0	0.061
2	0.425
4	0.980
6	1.213
8	1.646
10	2.158

5. Determine the linear equation that best fits this set of data. Plot the data points and this linear equation.

6. Determine the sum of the squares of the distances of these points from the best fit determined in problem 5.

7. Compare the error sum from problem 6 with the same error sum computed from the best quadratic fit. What do these sums tell you about the two models for the data?

Pipeline Flow Analysis. The friction in a circular pipeline causes a "velocity profile" to develop in the flowing oil. Oil that is in contact with the walls of the pipe is not moving at all, whereas the oil at the center of the flow is moving the fastest. The diagram in Figure 6.12 shows how the velocity of the oil varies across the diameter of the pipe and defines the variables used in this analysis. The following equation describes this velocity profile:

$$v(r) = v_{max}(1 - \frac{r}{r_0})^{1/n}$$

The variable n is an integer between 5 and 10 that defines the shape of the forward flow of the oil. In this case, the value of n for the diagram in Figure 6.12 is 8.

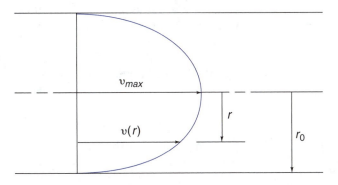

Figure 6.12 *Velocity profile in flowing oil.*

The average flow velocity of the pipe can be computed by integrating the velocity profile from zero to the pipe radius, r_0. Thus, we have

$$v_{ave} = \frac{\int_0^{r_0} v(r) 2\pi r \, dr}{\pi r_0^2}$$

$$= \frac{2 v_{max}}{r_0^2} \int_0^{r_0} r (1 - \frac{r}{r_0})^{1/n} dr$$

The values of v_{max} and n can be measured experimentally, and the value of r_0 is the radius of the pipe. For these problems, assume that v_{max} is 1.5 m, r_0 is 0.5 m, and n is 8.

8. Plot the function $r(1 - \frac{r}{r_0})^{1/n}$ for r, varying from 0 to 0.5 meters, in increments of 0.01 meters.

9. Approximate the area under the function in problem 8 using a triangle and a trapezoid as shown in Figure 6.13.

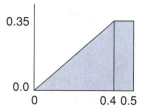

Figure 6.13 *Integral approximation.*

10. Compare your answer in problem 9 to the area of the function in problem 8 computed using the **quad** function.

11. What is the average flow velocity for this pipe?

12. Generate a table showing the average flow velocity for a pipeline, using the integer values of n from 5 to 10.

Function Analysis. Let the function f be defined by the following equation:

$$f(x) = 4e^{-x}$$

13. Plot this function over the interval [0,1]. Use numerical integration techniques to estimate the integral of $f(x)$ over [0,0.5] and over [0,1].

Sounding Rocket Trajectory. The following data represent the time and altitude values for a sounding rocket that is performing high-altitude atmospheric research on the ionosphere.

Time, s	Altitude, m
0	60
10	2,926
20	10,170
30	21,486
40	33,835
50	45,251
60	55,634
70	65,038
80	73,461
90	80,905
100	87,368
110	92,852
120	97,355
130	100,878
140	103,422
150	104,986
160	106,193
170	110,246
180	119,626
190	136,106
200	162,095
210	199,506
220	238,775
230	277,065
240	314,375
250	350,704

14. Plot the altitude data.

15. The velocity function is the derivative of the altitude function. Using numerical differentiation, compute the velocity values from these data, using a backward difference. Plot the velocity data. (Note that this is a two-stage rocket.)

16. The acceleration function is the derivative of the velocity function. Using the velocity data determined from problem 15, compute the acceleration data, using a backward difference. Plot the acceleration data.

Complete Solutions to Practice! Problems

SECTION 2.2, PAGE 24

1. 5 rows by 4 columns, or a 5x4 matrix
2. `G(2,2), G(4,1), G(4,2), G(4,4), G(5,4)`

SECTION 2.2, PAGE 26

1. 4×1
2. 2×3
3. 3×4
4. 1×7
5. 5×1
6. 2×1

SECTION 2.2, PAGE 30

1. `[1.5, 0.5, 8.2, 0.5, -2.3]'`
2. `[10, 11, 12, 13, 14, 15]`
3. `[4, 5, 6, 7, 8, 9; 1, 2, 3, 4, 5, 6]`
4. `[0, 0.1, 0.2, 0.3, 0.4, 0.5, 0.6, 0.7, 0.8, 0.9, 1.0]`
5. `[0.5, 0.5, 2.4; 1.2, -2.3, -4.5]`
6. `[0.6,1.5,2.3,-0.5; 5.7,8.2,9.0,1.5; 1.2,-2.3,-4.5,0.5]`

SECTION 2.3, PAGE 38

1. `factor = 1 + b/v + c/(v*v);`
2. `slope = (y2 - y1)/(x2 - x1);`
3. `resistance = 1/(1/r1 + 1/r2 + 1/r3);`
4. `loss = f*p*(1/d)*(v*v/2);`

SECTION 2.3, PAGE 41

1. `[2, -2, 1, 1]`
2. `[10, -4, 5, 0]`
3. `[0.6667, -0.5, -5, 0]`
4. `[8, 1, 0.2, 0]`
5. `[10, 3, 5.5, 16]`
6. `[4, -1.3333, -3.3333, 0]`

SECTION 3.1, PAGE 59

1. `-3`
2. `-2`
3. `-3`
4. `-2`
5. `-1`
6. `1`
7. `11`
8. `-1`
9. `[5, 4, 3, 2, 1, 0, 1, 2, 3, 4, 5]`
10. `[0, 0, 1, 1, 1, 2, 2, 1, 2, 3, 3, 4]`

SECTION 3.1, PAGE 60

1. `motion = sqrt(vi^2 + 2*a*x);`
2. `frequency = 1/sqrt((2*pi*c/L));`
3. `range = 2*vi*vi*sin(b)*cos(b)/g;`
4. `length = k*sqrt(1-(v/c)^2);`
5. `volume = 2*pi*x*x*((1-pi/4)*y-(0.8333-pi/4)*x);`
6. `center = 38.1972*(r^3 - s^3)*sin(a)/((r*r - s*s)*a);`

SECTION 3.2, PAGE 63

1. `7`
2. `[1, -1, -2]`
3. `[0, -1, -2, 7]`
4. `[2.3333, 3.3333, 3]`
5. `1.5`
6. `[1, 3 ,7; 2, 24, 28; 12, -24, -56]`
7. `[1, 3, 5, 21]`
8. `[1, -1, -2; 2, 3, 4; 6, 8, 7]`

SECTION 3.3, PAGE 68

1. `rand(1,10)*10;`
2. `rand(1,10)*2 - 1;`
3. `rand(1,10)*10 - 20;`
4. `rand(1,10)*0.5 + 4.5;`
5. `rand(1,10)*2*pi - pi;`

SECTION 3.5, PAGE 74

1. true
2. true
3. true
4. false
5. true
6. true
7. true
8. false

SECTION 3.5, PAGE 76

1.
```
if abs(volt_1 - volt_2) > 10
    fprintf('%f %f \n',volt_1, volt_2);
end
```

2.
```
if log(x) > 3
    time = 0;
    count = count + 1;
end
```

3.
```
if dist < 50 & time > 10
    time = time + 2;
else
    time = time + 2.5;
end
```

4.
```
if dist >= 100
    time = time + 2
elseif dist > 50
    time = time + 1
else
    time = time + 0.5
end
```

SECTION 3.5, PAGE 78

1. `[1, 1, 1];`
2. `[1, 3, 6, 7, 8]'`
3. `1`
4. `0`
5. `[1, 1, 1]'`
6. `[1, 0, 1]`

SECTION 3.5, PAGE 79

1. `18`
2. `17`
3. `9`
4. `11`
5. `0`
6. `4`

SECTION 4.1, PAGE 94

1. `[-1, 13]`
2. `[9, -7, 6; 7, -9, 10]`
3. `[39; -25; 18]`
4. `[1, 0; 0, 1]`
5. `[8, -4, 2; -2, 2, -2; 9, -3, 0];`
6. Does not exist
7. `64`
8. `0`

SECTION 4.2, PAGE 96

1. `[2,1]'`
2. `[0.3055, -0.5636, 1.0073]'`
3. `[2, 1, 3, -1]'`

SECTION 5.1, PAGE 105

1. `1/(x+4)/(x^2+8*x+16)`
2. `(x^2+8*x+16)*(x+4)^2`
3. `(x-2)/(x^2+8*x+16)`
4. `x^2+8*x+16`

SECTION 5.2, PAGE 106

1. `[2,1]'`
2. `[0.3055, -0.5636, 1.0073]'`
3. `[2, 1, 3, -1]'`

SECTION 5.3, PAGE 107

1. `3*x^2-10*x+2`

   `6*x-10`
2. `(2*x+4)*(x-1)+x^2+4*x+4`

   `6*x+6`
3. `(2*x-2)/(10*x-24)`

   `2/(10*x-24)`
4. `2*(x^5-4*x^4-9*x^3+32)*(5*x^4-16*x^3-27*x^2)`

   `2*(5*x^4-16*x^3-27*x^2)^2+2*(x^5-4*x^4-9*x^3+32)`
   `    *(20*x^3-48*x^2-54*x)`

SECTION 5.3, PAGE 108

1. `0.0550`
2. `0.5000`
3. `0.3750`
4. `0.2500`

SECTION 6.1, PAGE 116

1. ```
   t = 0:0.5:5;
   temp = [72.5, 78.1, 86.4, 92,3, 110.6, 111.5, 109.3, ...
           110.2, 110.5, 109.9, 110.2];
   new_t = 0:0.1:5;
   temp_linear = interp1(t,temp,new_t,'linear');
   temp_cubic = interp1(t,temp,new_t,'cubic');
   plot(new_t,temp_linear,new_t,temp_cubic,t,temp,'o'),
   title('Linear and Cubic Spline Interpolation'),
   xlabel('Time, s'),ylabel('Temperature, degrees F'),
   grid, pause
   ```
2. linear: `75.8600, 89.3500, 111.2480, 109.9240`

   cubic: `75.5360, 88.7250, 111.9641, 109.9081`
3. linear: `0.6747, 1.6011, 1.7104, 1.8743`

   cubic: `0.5449, 1.5064, 1.7628, 2.1474`

   (These answers used only the first six points so that the independent variable would be increasing.)
   ```

SECTION 6.3, PAGE 125

1. `0.0550`
2. `0.5000`
3. `0.3750`
4. `0.2500`

SECTION 6.5, PAGE 131

Assume that N is the number of points in the original function, **df1** contains the first derivative values, and **df2** contains the second derivative values. Then the points of local maxima and minima can be determined with these statements:

```
product = df1(1:N-2).*df1(2:N-1);
peaks   = find(product<0);
minima  = find(df2(peaks)>0.0001);
maxima  = find(df2(peaks)<-0.0001);
```

1. Local maxima occurs at these x values: 0.3000
   Local minima occurs at these x values: 3.2000
2. Local maxima occurs at these x values: none
   Local minima occurs at these x values: −1.9000
3. Local maxima occurs at these x values: none
   Local minima occurs at these x values: 1.1000
4. Local maxima occurs at these x values: none
   Local minima occurs at these x values: none
5. Local maxima occurs at these x values: −1.9000   2.1000
   Local minima occurs at these x values: −0.3000   3.7000

Index

MATLAB FUNCTION SUMMARY

This MATLAB summary lists all the special values, commands, and functions defined in this text.

abs	computes absolute value or magnitude
acos	computes arccosine
all	determines if all values are true
ans	stores expression value
any	determines if any values are true
asin	computes arcsine
atan	computes 2-quadrant arctangent
atan2	computes 4-quadrant arctangent
axis	controls axis scaling
ceil	rounds towards ∞
clc	clears command screen
clear	clears workspace
clf	clears figure
clock	represents the current time
collect	collects coefficient of a symbolic expression
cos	computes cosine of angle
cumprod	determines cumulative products
cumsum	determines cumulative sums
date	prints current date
demo	runs demonstrations
det	computes the determinant of a matrix
diff	differentiates a symbolic expression, also computes the differences between adjacent values
disp	displays matrix or text
else	optional clause in if structure
elseif	optional clause in if structure
end	defines end of a control structure
eps	represents floating-point precision
exit	terminates MATLAB
exp	computes value with base e
expand	expands a symbolic expression
eye	generates identity matrix
ezplot	generates a plot of a symbolic expression
factor	factors a symbolic expression
find	locates nonzero values
finite	determines if values are finite
fix	rounds towards zero
floor	rounds towards $-\infty$
for	generates loop structure
format +	sets format to plus and minus signs only
format compact	sets format to compact form
format long	sets format to long decimal
format long e	sets format to long exponential
format loose	sets format to non-compact form
format short	sets format to short decimal
format short e	sets format to short exponential
fprintf	prints formatted information
function	generates user-defined function
grid	inserts grid in a plot
help	invokes help facility
hist	plots histogram
horner	converts a symbolic expression into a nested form
i	represents the value $\sqrt{-1}$
if	tests logical expression
Inf	represents the value ∞
input	accepts input from keyboard
int	integrates a symbolic expression
interp1	computes linear and cubic interpolation
inv	computes the inverse of a matrix

`isempty`	determines if matrix is empty	`rem`	computes remainder from division
`isnan`	determines if values are NaNs	`round`	rounds to nearest integer
`j`	represents the value $\sqrt{-1}$	`save`	saves variables in a file
`length`	determines number of values in a vector	`semilogx`	generates a log-linear plot
		`semilogy`	generates a linear-log plot
`load`	loads matrices from a file	`sign`	generates $-1,0,1$ based on sign
`log`	computes natural logarithm	`simple`	shortens a symbolic expression
`log10`	computes common logarithm	`simplify`	simplifies a symbolic expression
`loglog`	generates a log-log plot	`sin`	computes sine of angle
`max`	determines maximum value	`size`	prints row and column dimensions
`mean`	determines mean value		
`median`	determines median value	`solve`	solves an equation
`min`	determines minimum value	`sort`	sorts values
`NaN`	represents the value Not-a-Number	`sqrt`	computes square root
		`std`	computes standard deviation
`numden`	returns the numerator and denominator expressions	`subplot`	splits graphics window into subwindows
`numeric`	converts a string to a number	`sum`	determines sum of values
`ones`	generates matrix of ones	`sym2poly`	converts a symbolic expression to a coefficient vector
`pause`	temporarily halts a program		
`pi`	represents the value π	`symadd`	adds two symbolic expressions
`plot`	generates a linear xy plot		
`poly2sym`	converts a vector to a symbolic polynomial	`symdiv`	divides two symbolic expressions
`polyfit`	computes a least-squares polynomial	`symmul`	multiplies two symbolic expressions
`polyval`	evaluates a polynomial	`sympow`	raises a symbolic expression to a power
`pretty`	prints a symbolic expression in typeset form	`symsub`	subtracts two symbolic expressions
`print`	print the graphics window	`symvar`	returns independent variable
`prod`	determines product of values	`tan`	computes tangent of angle
`quad`	computes the integral under a curve (Simpson)	`title`	adds a title to a plot
		`what`	lists variables
`quad8`	computes the integral under a curve (Newton-Cote)	`while`	generates a loop structure
		`who`	lists variables in memory
`quit`	terminates MATLAB	`whos`	lists variables in memory plus sizes
`rand`	generates a uniform random number		
		`xlabel`	adds x axis label to a plot
`randn`	generates a Gaussian random number	`ylabel`	adds y axis label to a plot
		`zeros`	generates matrix of zeros